ROYAL MISTRESSES

By the same author
Charles I: The Personal Monarch
Archbishop William Laud
Royal Childhoods

ROYAL MISTRESSES

CHARLES CARLTON

London and New York

First published 1990
by Routledge
Reprinted 1991
First published in paperback in 1991
by Routledge
11 New Fetter Lane, London EC4P 4EE
29 West 35th Street, New York, NY 10001

Typeset in 11/13pt Garamond by
Input Typesetting Ltd, London

Printed in Great Britain by
T J Press (Padstow) Ltd, Padstow, Cornwall

British Library Cataloguing in Publication Data
Carlton, Charles
Royal Mistresses.
1. Great Britain. Monarchs. Interpersonal relationships, history
I. Title
941'.009'92

Library of Congress Cataloging in Publication Data
Carlton, Charles
Royal mistresses / by Charles Carlton.
p.   cm.
1. Great Britain – Kings and rulers – Mistresses – Biography.
2. Favorites, Royal – Great Britain – Biography. 3. Mistresses – Great Britain –
Biography. I. Title.
DA308.C37   1991
941'.00992–dc20   90–26751
[B]

ISBN 0 415 00769 0 (hbk)
ISBN 0 415 06455 4 (pbk)

CONTENTS

PLATES

ACKNOWLEDGEMENTS

As usual I owe a debt of gratitude to Andrew Wheatcroft, my friend and editor at Routledge. I would like to thank Christa Howerton for editorial help and Kate Bostock for her invaluable work on the illustrations.

I am especially indebted to the following for permission to reproduce pictures from their collections: Joe Mitchenson of the Mander and Mitchenson Theatre Collection for Plates 18, 20, and 22; the Duke of Marlborough for Plate 15; and the Earl of Jersey for Plate 16. I am also grateful to the following for permission to reproduce pictures: Her Majesty the Queen for Plates 6, 8, 10, 11, and 23; Cambridge University Library for Plate 2; Giraudon for Plate 1; Mary Evans Picture Library for Plates 12, 19, 24, and 25 and the cover illustration; the National Portrait Gallery for Plates 4, 5, 7, 9, 13, 14, 17, and 21; Phaidon Press for Plate 3; and the Radio Times Hulton Picture Library for Plate 26.

I
'BE CIVIL. I AM THE PROTESTANT WHORE'

In January 1681 King Charles II summoned a parliament for the following March 21st. It was to meet in Oxford, not Westminster, the usual venue, for London was too hostile a place, and the political and religious conflicts that had wracked the kingdom for years were dangerously close to an explosive climax. The king moved first to Woodstock, a dozen miles north of the university, with his wife and two mistresses, Louise de Kéroüalle, the Duchess of Portsmouth, and Nell Gwynn, a spirited Londoner, who had started life as an orange-seller in the New Theatre. Even though the court tried to find diversion in horse racing – the sport which Charles II had turned into that of kings – signs of rising tension were apparent everywhere. Troops of soldiers lined the streets of the university city, through which partisans strutted with green satin ribbons in their hats proclaiming 'No Popery! No Slavery!' Gangs of roughs prowled about with steel-tipped staves, beating up their opponents. In St Mary's Church the two factions, which were to become the Whig and Tory parties, sat glaring at each other as they heard the word of God. Outside, the gutter press provided their version of His word in the most scurrilous fashion, portraying, for instance, the king's brother, the Catholic Duke of York as a half-Jesuit, half-devil, setting fire to London.

Everyone – everything – it seemed, was caught up in the political crisis. One afternoon, so the story goes, the mob saw a carriage with an attractive young woman inside, being driven towards the king's rooms. Believing it contained Charles's French Catholic mistress, Louise de Kéroüalle, the crowd surged towards the coach, and might have turned it over and done even worse damage to its occupant, had not the window opened to reveal Nell Gwynn, who, with her cockney, chirpy cheek shouted out, 'Pray, good people, be civil. I am the *Protestant* whore.'[1]

Pretty, witty Nell realized that throughout English history royal mistresses have had functions far wider than the mere sexual pleasure of the monarch. In this instance she had come to represent one of the two factions in a rapidly polarizing England. In many people's minds she was the Protestant mistress, who epitomized solid English virtues, in contrast to the Catholic, absolutist vices of Louis XIV's France. Thus a few days after Nell's profound quip, Charles had to reassure parliament he would 'never use arbitrary government', nor 'suffer it in others'.

While neither Nell Gwynn nor Louise de Kéroüalle exercised any real political power, they were totems around which political factions gathered, and they allowed the monarch to express his political preferences through his sexual options, particularly in the hot-house world of the royal court where events were so often personalized. Through his mistresses the king could not only proclaim a political preference, but by failing to do so, try to balance parties, and even play them one against the other so as to retain as much flexibility as possible.

This process was not, of course, one-way. Access to the ruler meant access to power, and there was no better way of getting the king's ear than spending the night asleep next to it. Since lovers of both sexes have been used to influence the monarch, in this book mistress will be applied to paramours of the same as well as the opposite sex. To use it only with regard to kept women would be to adhere to a linguistic double standard which does not apply to royal politics. Of course there were differences between male and female paramours. While both have been standard-bearers for political factions, women have usually acted for others, while men have more often become factional leaders with their own objectives. In doing so, male lovers have had to possess both considerable political skills as well as outstanding personal and sexual abilities. They need the former to overcome the venom society exhibits towards homosexuals (and rarely vents against heterosexual affairs). They require the latter to please the monarch and protect themselves from his subjects' wrath.

Until recent times the overwhelming majority of English kings selected their wives for political reasons. Before the twentieth century the only English monarch who married solely for love was Edward IV, and his choice of Elizabeth Woodville was politically disastrous. Occasionally monarchs fell in love with their wives after marrying them, as did Charles I with Henrietta Maria. More often they performed their dynastic duties adequately enough to sire male heirs, whilst finding sexual excitement and gratification elsewhere.

Since before Solomon's day kings have had harems of women, which have always been as much status symbols as they were sources of physical satisfaction. A man's power was measured in his possessions, and, in a society where women were seen as property, sexually possessing large numbers of them was the outward and visible sign of lordship. Although the feudal concept of *ius prima noctu* existed only in subjects' imaginations, it was an indication that in the world of sexual fantasy the right to possess each dependent woman's maidenhead was the ultimate lordship. From the Sabines to the Red Army's capture of Berlin, the rape of the enemy's women was the ultimate act of conquest. And, in much the same fashion, from Henry I's casual couplings with peasant girls to Edward VII's teatime dalliances with the wives of the aristocracy, the possession of many women was an obvious sign of a prince's political and sexual potency.

A regal extra-marital relationship could also be symbolic of a political alliance, which demonstrated that the monarch was intimately linked with a particular party, faction or policy. Just as the crudest description for the sexual act may also be used as a verb to convey the overwhelming use of power, so the phrase 'being in bed with' implies a close political liaison.[2]

Kings could afford to support bevies of bastards, who were unlikely to become a burden on their subjects who paid the poor rate, and have thus always regarded illegitimacy more of an economic problem than a moral one. Mistresses seldom practised birth control, if only because having the king's child, particularly a son, greatly enhanced their status and gave them a long-term link with the crown. Anyway, even if they had wanted to avoid pregnancy, and had their lovers taken precautions, contemporary medical knowledge on the subject was far from efficacious. One suspects that the main contraceptive consequence of the advice of Albertus Magnus, the thirteenth-century Dominican scientist, to spit thrice in a frog's mouth, eat bees, or drink sheep's urine or hare's blood beforehand, was to dissuade most couples from making love in the first place. None the less, as Henry Kissinger once observed: 'Power is the great aphrodisiac.'

1 *The Fall of Man*, from the Burgundian Book of Hours painted for the Duc de Berri about 1410 (Giraudon/Musée de Chantilly)

Sexual adventures were, too, great escapes for many of a monarch's subjects, particularly as the crown lost real power. Conducted with panache, taste, and a decent respect for each other, a monarch's affairs may become fantasies for his people. Nude paintings of Charles II's mistresses poured from the studios of court artists such as Sir Peter Lely, to satisfy the prurient interests of loyal subjects, while Pepys recorded a dream ('the best that ever was') of sleeping with Barbara Palmer, one of the most attractive of the king's paramours.[3] Two centuries later ordinary working men cheered Edward VII when, with an attractive young woman in tow, he celebrated his horse winning the Derby. On the other hand a monarch who flaunted his promiscuity, particularly when he directed it towards members of his own sex, ran the grave risk of offending his largely heterosexual subjects. He could lose popularity and effectiveness, as did James I. Should his conduct become too blatant and odious he might well, like Edward II, suffer deposition and an excruciatingly painful end.

In contrast, illicit love can increase the monarch's power because unlike a wife or legitimate children, lovers and bastards are utterly dependent on the king. Thus a monarch's paramours have tended to come from the middling ranks of society, the sons and daughters of merchants and country gentry. Common folk lacked the manners to survive for long in a royal court, while the dangers of forming a liaison with the wife or daughter of a magnate were immense. One of the complaints against King John was that he seduced the high-born and well-connected. It was bruited that when Robert FitzWalter's daughter refused to sleep with him he destroyed her father's castle, forced him into exile, and poisoned her. Others said that Eustace de Vesci became a leader of the baronial revolt that produced Magna Carta because John had propositioned his wife. John and Henry VIII were the only two English kings who took the political risk of divorce – or rather annulling their marriages. Since queens were normally chosen to cement a political alliance, to make a peace treaty, or for their very large dowries, they invariably came from powerful families, who could be extremely upset by the insult of divorce.

While it might have been difficult and dangerous to divorce a wife, it was impossible to disinherit a lawfully begotten heir – if only because such went against the fundamental principal of monarchy, the legitimate passage of the crown from one generation to another which, while not assuring ability, avoided the far worse catastrophe of a disputed succession and civil war.

It did of course create other problems within the royal family. A legitimate heir enjoys a great deal of independence, because, no matter what he does his father cannot disinherit him. Thus while George II might quarrel publicly with his heir, once coming to fisticuffs with the Prince of Wales when they happened to meet at the theatre, he could not be rid of the boy. The thought that one day he could inherit his father's throne exacerbated the usual Oedipal tensions between father and son. In myth the ancient Greeks portrayed Oedipus as a prince who wanted to possess his father's throne as well as his father's wife. In real life, many heirs recognized, consciously or not, that by wanting to succeed to the throne, and thus fulfilling their roles as adults, they were also wishing for the king's death, and were thus guilty of wanting to commit both patricide and regicide.

Mistresses and bastards had no rights and few expectations. Every night the former had to prove their position: every day the latter must demonstrate their fidelity. The emotional problems suffered by those who lacked a legal foundation for their relationships to the ruler could well be intensely painful – as William the Conqueror discovered. On the other hand, the king often found satisfaction in the illegitimacy of others. For instance, during the twelfth century Henry I, who had over twenty bastards, used his daughters to make marriage alliances, and his sons as loyal servants – if only because they were his dependants. Fifty years later, after his wife and legitimate sons rose up and rebelled against him, the sole person Henry II could completely trust was his bastard, Geoffrey Plantagenet. 'You alone have proved yourself my lawful and true son', the dying king told him, 'my other sons are really the bastards.'[4]

Lovers, wives, catamites, children, bastards, divorce, sexuality – all of these touch on the deepest desires and passions that human beings possess. These drives are the reason for our survival as a species, the core of our very being. Thus an examination of a monarch's illicit life sheds light on his character and reign. It was no coincidence that Henry I, Charles II, and Edward VII, who were successful with their mistresses, were also successful in their reigns, while the divorced John and the love-lorn Edward VIII failed.

So it is not surprising that the affairs of the sovereign's heart have very often become the affairs of state. When kings do foolish things for their lovers – be they male or female – then as James I, Edward II, or Edward VIII proved, kingdoms quake. When the succession is uncertain, as William Rufus and Henry II realized, civil war could all too often be the result. If kings felt guilty about their sexual affairs, or if those affairs disgusted their subjects, the repercussions could, as Edward II and James II painfully discovered, be catastrophic.

Guilt and illicit passion have played their parts in shaping the history of the English crown. William's illegitimacy helped to bring about the conquest, John's reputation for debauchery in part resulted in the sealing of Magna Carta, Henry VIII's lusts were integral in precipitating the Reformation, while James II's sense of his own sexual sinfulness may well have helped turn 1688 into the Bloodless, as well as the Glorious Revolution. If by the eighteenth century the position of royal mistress had become almost formalized, their presence also helped the development of the office of Prime Minister, for they acted as links between the Palace and Downing Street. Since the eighteenth century the crown has lost power: it reigns rather than rules. In recent times Edward VIII's inability to come to terms with both his libido and the limits democracy imposes on a constitutional monarch have done much to shape the monarchy we know today.

II

'NOTHING IS MORE VILE THAN TO
LOVE A WIFE LIKE A MISTRESS'

Before the Norman Conquest stories of royal mistresses and illicit love were shrouded in myth, confused by the lack of clear-cut definitions of marriage and legitimacy, compounded by the lack of evidence, and exaggerated through fantasy. Bastard sons were supposed to have inherited their father's thrones, particularly after the death of all their legitimate half-brothers. Ethelbad, King of the West Saxons from 855 to 860, married his father's second wife and widow, Judith, perhaps because he wanted to maintain an alliance with her father Charles the Bald, King of the Franks. In the ancient kingdom of Bernicai – where apparently no one bothered to count illegitimate girls – King Ida (547–99) was supposed to have produced twelve bastard sons, King Ethelfrith (592–616) five, and King Oswiu (641–70) a rather parsimonious one. Many believed that Ecgwynn, the first wife of Edward the Elder, King Alfred's heir, was in fact his concubine, and that Edward the Elder should not have inherited his father's throne in 899. The same allegation of concubinage was also made against Wulthryth, second wife of Edgar, King of England from 959 to 975. Often a royal pretender would try to blacken the reputation of rivals by asserting that their mother had in fact been a concubine.

Although the church had not defined clearly the state of marriage, many misogynous monks drew no distinction between legal and illicit sex. 'Nothing is more vile than to love a wife like a mistress', declared St Jerome.[1] When the English missionary St Boniface, a constant critic of sexual license by both kings and commoners, heard in 746 that Aethelbad, King of Mercia, had taken a legal wife, he wrote reproving him for being so 'governed by lust', that he had committed 'the sin of lasciviousness and adultery'. Doubtless Boniface, who frequently fulminated about

2 *The royal bed*, from Trinity College MS.o.9.34 (Cambridge University Library)

royal promiscuity, saw the workings of Providence when ten years later Aethelbad was murdered by his own bodyguard.[2] Towards the end of the Anglo-Saxon period the church took an increasingly obdurate stand against unions that it had not blessed, and which it believed were becoming rife amongst the upper classes. In 786, for instance, a legatine commission recommended that all children 'begotten in adultery or incest', should not be allowed to inherit from their fathers.[3] Thus it is not surprising that the wildest of stories about royal mistresses developed. The one that Aelgifu was the *concubina regis* first of Ethelred the Unready, (978–1016), then of his obdurate enemy Canute (1016–35), and finally of Canute's son Harold Harefoot (1037–40), is clearly impossible for reasons of chronology, if not common decency.

The Aelgifu that Ethelred married was the daughter of either Earldorman Ethelbert or Earldorman Thored. Since she had ten surviving children before she died, permitting her husband to remarry in 1002, she could well have been born in the early 960s.

Canute's Aelgifu is generally regarded to have been his mistress. She was the daughter of Earldorman Aelfred of Northampton, whose loyalty to the Saxon monarchs was so dubious that they blinded two of his sons. Thus it is not surprising that Aelgifu became the mistress of one of the leaders of the invading Vikings, Olaf, King of Norway – nicknamed 'The Saint' – from whom she was captured by Canute. He had two sons by her, Swend and Harold Harefoot, before taking a wife, Emma, the widow of his vanquished Saxon enemy, Ethelred the Unready. This marriage could well have persuaded the proud and ambitious Aelgifu to go with her son Swend to try to rule Norway, from whence they were expelled by Magnus, Olaf's son.

Harold Harefoot, who inherited the kingdom of England from his father, Canute, formed an irregular liaison with a woman also called Aelgifu. He fought a civil war with his legitimate half-brother, Harthacnut, which ended with Harold's death in 1040, and Harthacnut's accession to the English throne.

Less obscure, and even more tragic, was the story of Eadgyth Swannheshals, or Edith of the Swan-neck, who was the concubine of Harold Godwinson, Duke of Wessex, later King Harold II. Whilst Harold was Earl of Wessex she lived happily with him, having at least six children, one of whom, Gytha, married Waldemar, King of Novgorod (now in Russia), while another Gunhild became a nun closer to home at Wilton. But in early 1066 King

Edward the Confessor died. He was so pious a man that he refused to consummate his marriage. While the church – which never really approved of sex within or without wedlock – was impressed enough to canonize the king, and name Westminster Abbey in his honour, Edward's self-restraint left England with a serious succession problem. Harold of Wessex immediately seized the throne by having Archbishop Earldred of York crown him King of England on 6 January. Realizing that he would have to fight to keep the throne, Harold hurriedly looked around for allies. He jettisoned Edith, his mistress, to marry Edith, the well-connected sister of Edwin, Earl of Mercia and of Morca, Earl of Northumberland.

This alliance kept the North loyal, enabling Harold to defeat the invasion led by Harold Hardrada, King of Norway, and by his own brother, Tosti, at Stamford Bridge on 25 September 1066. But his new marriage was not efficacious enough to prevent his defeat and death at the Battle of Hastings on 14 October. William the Conqueror's victory was so decisive, and the piles of slain Anglo-Saxon corpses were so high, that Harold's mutilated body could only be identified by Edith of the Swan-neck, who recognized an intimate birthmark that only a lover could know for sure.

The repercussions of the Norman Conquest were profound: it established links with the continent as opposed to Scandinavia, it modified the language, strengthened feudalism, and destroyed the Anglo-Saxon order, replacing it with a new Norman elite. In all, there was hardly a person in the realm that the conquest did not effect. Yet it was essentially one man, William the Bastard, Duke of Normandy, who brought about this revolution.

As the name by which Duke William is known in French history suggests, the most important feature about the conqueror's life was his illegitimate birth. According to a twelfth-century chronicler, one fine morning Robert, Duke of Normandy, saw Herleve (sometimes known as Arlette) washing clothes in the stream that ran beside his castle at Falaise. It was a case of love, or at least lust, at first sight. Quite literally sweeping her off her feet, he carried her back to his chamber where that night they conceived a child, William, who was born in about 1028. Since the church had not blessed his parents' romantic union, the baby had slight expectations until 1034, when Robert impetuously decided to go

3 *Aelgyva and a clergyman,* from the Bayeux Tapestry recording William the Conqueror's victory over the Saxons in 1066. The naked figure below suggests an embarrassing Saxon scandal (Phaidon Press)

off to the Holy Land on a crusade, and persuaded his barons to accept the boy as his heir just in case he failed to return.

After Robert died in Nicea in Asia Minor on the way home, the barons reneged on their promise to accept William as their duke, and Normandy drifted into a terrible civil war. Rape, looting, and plunder infested the land. It was as if the Vikings had returned to ply their terrible ways. Factions fought each other as they all tried to seize the heir. Two of his tutors, Gilbert and Turold, were assassinated, while his steward, Osbern, died in an affray fought in the boy's own bedroom. Often his uncle Walter had to spend the night on guard in the young duke's room, and on several occasions they had to flee hurriedly from baronial coups, taking refuge in some peasant's hovel.

In 1046, when William came of age, a group of barons led by Guy of Burgundy tried to seize him. Warned, he escaped, and after a desperate ride, managed to ford the Vire estuary at low tide, eluding his pursuers to find refuge with Henry I. The French king invaded Normandy the following year, and routed the rebellious barons, led by Guy of Burgundy, at the Battle of Val-es-Dunes. It took William another dozen years to completely consolidate his rule, and it was not until he defeated his old ally, Henry I, at the Battle of Mortemer, in 1054, that he was completely secure.

Thus his decision twelve years later to invade England and risk all that he had won after so many decades of turmoil is a remarkable one, particularly as the conquest, a landing by a small amphibious force, sailing against the prevailing winds, with little possibility of reinforcements, was a desperate gamble. He invaded England because he was firmly convinced that once again a perfidious baron was trying to deprive him of his rightful patrimony.

Bastardy is a cruel rejection. Having had his pleasure of Herleve, Robert cast her aside, marrying her off in 1030 to one of his barons, Heluin, Vicomte of Conteville. With equal irresponsibility he rejected Normandy by leaving for the crusade that resulted in his own premature death, and nearly a generation of civil war.

Although illegitimacy was not as great a stigma in the early middle ages as it was to become later, William felt the burden of the bar sinister keenly. When, as a young man trying to regain his inheritance, he was taunted by the defenders of Alencon Castle waving hides and skins and shouting 'Hides for the tanner! Hides for the tanner!', he felt this as a mortal insult since his maternal grandfather had pursued that humble trade, and extracted a terrible revenge. One story tells how, having captured the castle, he punished the garrison by amputating all their limbs; or, relates another, skinning them alive. William blamed the civil wars of his youth on the circumstances of his birth. 'Calling me a bastard, degenerate, and unworthy to reign', he fulminated, Guy of Burgundy 'strove to strip me of the whole of Normandy.' His relatives, he complained 'treated me with contempt as a bastard'. The experience taught him never to trust anyone fully, to be ruthless in his goals, and to insist on receiving everything that was his by right. 'My nearest friends, my own kindred, who ought to have defended me at all hazards against the whole world formed conspiracies against me, and nearly stripped me of the inheritance of my fathers', recalled the Duke.[4]

Thus when Harold seized the English throne in early 1066, depriving him of the inheritance that William was convinced the Earl of Wessex had promised to help him obtain after being shipwrecked in France in 1051, the duke's anger was boundless. Immediately he sent messengers urging Harold 'to desist from this mad policy', and assembled an army and fleet to regain his rightful kingdom. William was utterly convinced that Edward the Confessor had nominated him as his successor, through his descent from King Ethelred and his second wife Emma.

William was renowned for being faithful to his own wife, Matilda, and treated priests who took mistresses with unusual severity. William of Poitiers, the official Norman historian of the invasion made much of the fact that Harold was wicked enough to have a mistress. The Conqueror knew only too well the psychological costs that illicit love can inflict on its innocent offspring.

In contrast, William I's third son, Henry I, who ruled England from 1100 to 1135, took advantage of the insecurity and dependency that mistresses and their progeny feel. An effective king, ready to listen to people, he expected obedience. Ruthless and cruel, he was a man of moderate appetites – except where sex was concerned, for he fathered some twenty illegitimate children by about a dozen women. None of his mistresses had any influence over policy, with the possible exception of Nest, daughter of the Prince of South Wales, by whom he had a son. So fair was she that she became known as 'the Helen of Wales', and like that mythical Greek beauty her abduction led to war. When Owain, son of Cadwgan ap Bleddyn, kidnapped her and her son by Henry, the English king was so angry that he invaded Ceredigion.

Henry made good unions for his bastards. Sybil married Alexander I, King of the Scots, Maud wed Rotrou, Count of Perche, while another daughter, also named Maud, married Conan III, Duke of Brittany. Not only were his daughters useful pawns whom he used to cement political alliances, but his sons were loyal dependants whom he employed to execute his policies. In return he made Robert Earl of Gloucester, and Rainald Earl of Cornwall. Even though in middle age Henry may have had a crisis of conscience about philandering, for he gave a large number of bequests to nunneries in 1130–1, by siring illegitimate children who could not inherit he seems to have been trying to avoid the problems that had bedevilled his own inheritance.

When William the Conqueror died in 1087, he left the Duchy of Normandy to his eldest son, Robert, England to his second, William Rufus, and miscellaneous estates and possessions to his third, Henry. The concept of primogeniture, by which the eldest son inherited the whole estate, to prevent its fragmentation and fratricidal conflict, was not yet developed. So immediately after William was killed in a hunting accident in the New Forest in August 1100, Henry seized the English throne, and had himself crowned king. Quite understandably Robert objected, and tried to invade England, but was repulsed. In 1106 Henry landed in Normandy, beating Robert at the Battle of Tincebrai, where he was captured, to remain in prison for the rest of his life.

Thus it is not surprising that Henry decided to limit himself to having only one legitimate male heir, William, so as to avoid a disputed succession. Unfortunately all his plans came to naught on the night of 25 November 1120.

Earlier that day Henry set out from the port of Harfleur in Normandy to return to England, leaving behind his only legitimate son, William, carousing with some friends. By the time the heir left, not only he and his companions were drunk, but so too were most of the crew of the *White Ship*, the fastest vessel in the Royal Navy. Even though it was a clear and relatively calm evening, the helmsman hit a rock at the harbour mouth and the vessel started to flounder. William was put on one of the ship's boats. As he was being rowed away to safety the heir heard the cries of his bastard half-sister, Maud, Countess of Perche. He ordered the boat's crew to return to pick her up, but panic-stricken swimmers in the water swamped the vessel. Everyone, including William, Maud, and another half-brother Richard, was drowned, except for a butcher from Rouen, who survived by tying himself to the mast.

To repair this terrible loss Henry two months afterwards married Adela of Louvain, but she proved barren. So the king had to make do with his only remaining legitimate child, Matilda, an intelligent, resolute, and energetic person, who suffered from one glaring defect – she was a woman. The barons were loath to accept a female ruler. Of course, they promised to do so on at least three occasions when Henry forced them to take oaths of allegiance, but the moment he died in 1135 many of them broke their word, and a civil war between Matilda and Stephen (who was William the Conqueror's grandson) ravaged England until the accession of Henry II in 1154 brought stability back again to the land.

Ironically, the law and order that Henry II restored broke down because of a surplus of legitimate heirs: the king had three sons – Henry, Richard, and John – all of whom were urged to rebel against their father by a mother, Eleanor of Aquitaine, determined on revenge.

Eleanor of Aquitaine was a remarkable woman, whose personality has survived the test of ages. Born the duchess of a large and rich province, she married Louis VII when she was only fifteen. Although they had two daughters their marriage did not work. He became moody and monkish, going off on a crusade; she devoted herself to the fantasies of courtly love. Although Eleanor accompanied her husband on his crusade she may well have allowed her love for his fellow knights in Christ to go beyond the merely platonic. Anyway, in 1152 Louis VII had the Pope annul their marriage, whereupon she married her ex-husband's rival, Henry of Anjou, a virile man eleven years her junior, who inherited the English throne two years later. At first her second marriage was a happy one that produced eight children, but by the birth of the last, John, on Christmas Eve 1167, it had broken down. If John's conception had been the result of a last desperate coupling to rescue a sinking marriage it failed.

Rosamund, the daughter of Sir Walter Clifford of Bredelais on the Welsh Borders, found a home in the ruins of Henry's marriage, becoming his mistress in 1173 when she was about sixteen. Rosamund was reputed to be the love of the king's life. When she died in 1176 he was distraught, giving several large bequests to the nuns of Godstow, Oxfordshire, who buried her under their church choir, just in front of the altar. After her sudden death Rosamund became something of a cult figure. The nuns of Godstow so venerated her that when Bishop Hugh of Lincoln visited their peaceful nunnery beside the River Thames in 1191 he was shocked to find her tomb adorned with rich silks, lamps and fine wax candles. 'She was a harlot', fulminated the bishop as he ordered Rosamund exhumed and buried elsewhere.[5] The bishop's indignation lent credence to the rumour that he was in fact Henry II's son by an early mistress. Anyway, the nuns obeyed, reinterring Rosamund in their chapter house, where she remained until the Reformation, when an even greater intolerance caused her to be dug up again and scattered to the four winds.

Over the centuries this romantic woman – who was known as 'Fair Rosamund' – became the focus for a host of legends. According to one of the earliest, recorded nearly two centuries after her death, Queen Eleanor tried to murder her young rival by having her bleed to death in a hot bath. A later legend recounted that the old queen managed to find a way into the maze that Henry had built at Woodstock to protect his mistress by following a silk thread which laid a trail from a sewing basket taken in to the young woman. Confronting her, Eleanor supposedly offered Rosamund the choice of either drinking a bowl of poison or killing herself with a dagger.

While neither of these stories was literally true, they do suggest a degree of popular sympathy for 'Fair Rosamund' that contrasts markedly with the increasingly harsh stand that the church was taking against illicit love, as well as a surprising amount of venom between Queen Eleanor and the king's mistress. Younger mistresses were an expected price that older queens paid for the position, status and wealth that marriage gave them. Eleanor knew full well that her husband was notoriously promiscuous, producing at least two bastards, Geoffrey Plantagenet, Archbishop of York, and William Longsword, Earl of Gloucester.

Although Henry's affair with Rosamund did not cause his estrangement from Eleanor, it almost certainly made their relationship more bitter, and explains why she encouraged her sons to rebel against their father, and why Henry, having defeated their rebellion, imprisoned his wife until his death in 1189. But locking mother up only encouraged her children to try to destroy father. After the king attempted to divide his two surviving legitimate sons, Richard and John, by threatening to leave all his dominions to the latter, the boys allied with King Philip Augustus of France and forced Henry to accept their terms. As he lay dying, his bastard but faithful son, Geoffrey Plantagenet, read out the rebels' names. 'Can it be true', exclaimed the king on hearing the first, 'that John, my heart, whom I have loved more than all my other sons, has forsaken me? Read no more. I care not for myself or the world.'[6]

Henry II quarrelled with his legitimate children because he could never allow them to become fully independent. He loved them, and as young children kept them with him whenever possible as he travelled through his dominions, which he boasted (with not too much exaggeration) extended from the Pyrenees to the Arctic Ocean. He kept on promising them lands and honours, but as they grew older was reluctant to make such gifts, since they would give them an independent power base. Unlike his legitimate sons, his bastards, such as Geoffrey Plantagenet, whom he called his only true son, had no claim to a patrimony, and thus had to remain dependent on their father.

By now the church was taking a far harder line against illicit sexual relations, by defining marriage more precisely as an indissoluble union between two consenting adults. Because incest was the most common excuse for annulment, in 1215 Rome restricted the prohibited degree of relations from sixth to fourth cousins. It also attempted to prevent annulments on the grounds of having previously promised to marry someone else by insisting that the banns be read out beforehand, and that all weddings take place as publicly as possible, either in front of the church door, or inside the church itself. Two decades later common law ruled that children born outside wedlock should never inherit, not even when their parents subsequently married.

As far as the royal family was concerned these changes made themselves felt in two ways. First, the concept of legitimate accession became far more widely accepted, particularly as the institutions of monarchy became stronger. Second, public opinion grew less tolerant of extra-marital activities, both heterosexual and homosexual ones, particularly if the monarch enjoyed them without public restraint.

Although Richard I spent the vast majority of his reign from 1189 to 1199 outside England, either on a crusade or putting down rebellions in his French dominions, the crown none the less managed to retain much of the power Henry II had won. Rumours of an affair with Raife de Clermont, a young knight whom he had rescued from Saracen capitivity, did nothing to tarnish the Lionheart's reputation as the epitome of medieval chivalry.

During the turbulent reign of Richard's successor the barons became so outraged by John's failed policies and outrageous behaviour (which many believed included attempting to seduce the wives and daughters of the high born – those of the common folk were fair game) that they forced him to seal Magna Carta in 1215. None the less the royal succession had become so secure that when John died the following year, his son, Henry III, succeeded without a civil war, even though he was only nine, and after he died in 1272 Edward I was able to remain abroad for two years before returning to take up the English throne.

The establishment of legitimate inheritance did not mean that a king could do what he wished once he came to the throne. The reign of Edward II (1307–27), demonstrated that a monarch could not flaunt an illicit relationship, particularly one which offended the moral and political susceptibilities of the barons.

Edward was not the first homosexual king of England – neither would he be the last. For instance, two centuries earlier William Rufus, son of William I, surrounded himself with effeminate young men whose long hair, gaudy clothes, and mincing gait offended the clerics who wrote the histories of his reign. But intense relationships between men were not unusual in the single-sex world of feudal knighthood, where knights might rescue a young maid only to desert her for the dragons of unnatural vice. As William Rufus's most recent biographer has observed, in Norman society 'sodomy was rife' and his eldest brother, Robert, Duke of Normandy was most probably a bisexual.[7] In fact Rufus's sexual preferences did not offend his contemporaries as much as they did nineteenth-century historians. One of them was convinced that Rufus's 'life reveals the depth to which a man can sink', while another, a deeply patriotic Oxford don, added 'In him England might see on his own soil the habits of the ancient Greek and modern Turk.'[8] At the time, however, chroniclers such as Eadmer, the monk from Canterbury, found William's rape of the church far more offensive than that of his fellow men.

But two hundred years later, by the reign of Edward II, the church had done much to change attitudes toward homosexuality, having, for instance, employed allegations of unnatural depravity to destroy the Order of the Knights Templar.[9] More serious, Edward openly violated accepted standards, particularly with his paramour, Piers Gaveston, and lacked those virile virtues such as endurance or courage that William Rufus undeniably possessed, and which Richard the Lionheart personified. Edward II liked brick-laying, plastering, and thatching: humble trades best left to low-born folk. He delighted in rowing and swimming – sissy sports, well beneath the dignity of martial aristocrats.

Such tastes contrasted markedly with those of his father, Edward I, a virile warrior who was so busy conquering the Welsh and defeating the Scots that he spent little time at home with his son, and thus failed to become a strong masculine role-model for the boy. Prince Edward had a particularly lonely childhood. His parents left him in England when he was two to go to France where his mother died fifteen months later. That same year his grandmother, Eleanor of Provence, passed away, and since his father remained single for ten years, no step-mother ever filled the void in the boy's life. His father neither liked his son, nor the company he kept. In June 1305 he banished the lad and his friend Piers Gaveston from court, allegedly for poaching some of the Bishop of Coventry's deer, a particularly harsh punishment for what on the surface seems a youthful prank. Even though the king allowed them back three months later, and permitted them to join his campaign against the Scots, he remained deeply suspicious of his son's relations with the young Frenchman. When the prince asked him in early 1307 to make Gaveston Count of Ponthieu the king, surely suspicious of their relationship, became very angry. 'You base-born whoreson', Edward I shouted, tearing a handful of hair from his son's head.[10] He expelled the lad from court, and banished Gaveston from the realm.

Five months later when Edward I died, one of the new king's first acts was to recall Gaveston to England, where his influence grew nearly as precipitously as his arrogance. 'I do not remember to have heard that one man so loved another', recorded one chronicler.[11] Another explained that, on first seeing Piers, Edward 'fell so much in love that he entered upon an enduring compact with him, and chose and determined to knit an unbreakable bond of affection with him, before all other mortals'. The new king disgraced Gaveston's enemies, Ralph Baldock, Bishop of London, and Walter Langton, Bishop of Coventry, and awarded the latter's forfeit estate, valued at some £50,000, as well as £100,000 collected for a crusade, to the favourite. In August he created Gaveston Earl of Cornwall. In October 1307 he married him to Margaret de Clare, his niece, less – one suspects – for her physical attributes, than for her expectations as the Earl of Gloucester's heiress. When the king went to France in January 1308 to marry Isabella, Philip IV's daughter, he made Gaveston Regent. Afterwards, at the coronation, the favourite offended the barons by wearing a sumptuous pearl-dripping robe of purple (the colour reserved for royalty). At the ensuing banquet the king displayed far more interest in Gaveston than in his new bride, and afterwards presented Piers with the best of Isabella's jewels and wedding presents. A contemporary described the upstart's demeanour towards the aristocracy; 'He lorded it over them like a second king.'[12]

When Edward's first parliament assembled in April 1308 the barons were determined to take their revenge, and demanded that Gaveston be banished. With great reluctance the king agreed to send him to Ireland as his Lord Lieutenant. But he escorted Piers to Bristol where he took ship for Dublin. During his friend's absence Edward did his utmost to ensure his return, by mending fences with powerful aristocrats, seeking the French king's support, and even writing to the Pope to have him rescind the order issued by Archbishop Winchelsey excommunicating Gaveston if he ever set foot again in England. After the Holy Father forgave the catamite, and several barons came over to the king's side, Edward felt confident enough to recall the favourite. But Gaveston's time in Ireland had made him even more insufferable, if only because he had been unusually effective in dealing with the turbulent Irish. He composed insulting nicknames for the leading aristocrats, who in September 1311 forced the king to banish him once again.

By Christmas Gaveston was back at court. According to Christopher Marlowe, Queen Isabella complained that:

> *The king regards me not,*
> *But dotes upon the love of Gaveston.*
> *He claps his cheek, and hangs about his neck,*
> *Smiles in his face, and whispers in his ears.*

Outraged by such indecent behaviour, and fearful what schemes the favourite might be whispering into the royal ear, the barons, led by

Thomas, Earl of Lancaster, rose in revolt. Archbishop Winchelsey excommunicated the favourite. Gaveston's property was seized and he was forced to take refuge in Scarborough Castle. Unfortunately the favourite omitted to provision this stronghold, which after a fortnight he had to surrender to the Earl of Pembroke, who took him to Deddington, Oxfordshire. Here Lords Lancaster, Hereford, and Arundel shanghaied him, and after a kangaroo court martial, beheaded him on Blacklow Hill, just outside the town of Warwick.

For several days the headless corpse lay on the cold earth, prey to scavengers, until four cobblers retrieved it. Using their professional skills they sewed the head back on, and brought Gaveston to Oxford where the king had him buried with great ceremony.

Distraught, Edward II bided his time, secretly plotting revenge. He improved relations sufficiently with his wife to produce four children, after which he fell under the influence of Hugh Despenser, the son and heir of the Earl of Winchester, one of the few magnates who stood by the king during the Gaveston affair. Edward's relations with the younger Despenser were almost certainly not platonic, as evidenced by the harsh reaction they produced from the queen and other barons. Ignoring the Earl of Pembroke's warnings that 'he perished on the rocks that loves another more than himself', in 1318 Edward made Hugh Chancellor of England, and supported the Despensers' efforts to expand their estates in the Welsh Marches. This so threatened the neighbouring Marcher Lords that it prompted a rebellion in which Thomas, Earl of Lancaster, forced the king to banish both Despensers in 1321. In its turn, aristocratic arrogance produced a backlash that enabled the king to capture Lancaster, whom he executed in March 1322, in a ceremony that almost parodied Gaveston's death.

The following year Roger Mortimer, Lancaster's son, escaped from the Tower of London by plying his guards with drugged wine. He fled to France, where a couple of years later Queen Isabella joined him. Soon the two became lovers. In 1326 they landed on the Suffolk coast with an invasion force, and with little difficulty persuaded the panic-stricken king to surrender and renounce the throne in favour of his son, Edward III. The Despensers were captured, and executed in a barbaric fashion, Hugh the younger being castrated before being disembowelled, because, as Froissart, the chronicler explained, 'he was a heretic and a sodomite'.[13] For a while Edward was held prisoner in Berkeley Castle. After being freed, and then recaptured, Isabella and Roger had the ex-king murdered, almost certainly by having his innards burnt out with a red hot poker inserted through his anal orifice.

Behind this horrid story of intrigue and brutal murders lay a web of illicit love and unnatural vices. While not the first English queen to be deceived, Isabella was the only one to become the lover of her husband's mortal enemy – perhaps because the manner by which her husband betrayed her was the most insulting any woman could suffer. It certainly explains the fashion of her husband's murder. Edward was hated not just because he allowed his catamites to come out of the closet, but because he installed them prominently in the centre of the royal council chamber, where they insulted those proud men who believed that they, and not some jumped up French faggot, were the natural leaders of late feudal society. If it was Gaveston and Despenser's arrogance which alienated the barons, it was their open immorality that offended English public opinion, which at the end of the middle ages, as the papacy grew more corrupt, was becoming less tolerant.

Such a shift Alice Perrers, Edward III's mistress, discovered to her cost. The calumny that she was the daughter of a tiler from Essex and a domestic skivvy, seems unlikely, for such a low birth would disqualify her from becoming a bed-chamber woman to Queen Philippa. It seems that she came from a family of Hertfordshire gentry, and entered the king's bed in about 1366, when the royal accounts record that Edward III gave her two tuns of wine. This gift was the first of many. Alice was a notoriously acquisitive and combative woman, who shocked male sensitivity by personally pleading before the courts at Westminster. Following Queen Philippa's death in 1369 and Edward's subsequent descent into senility, her domination of the king increased all the more. Edward gave her the manor of Wendover, many of his late wife's jewels, and an annuity worth £100. So rich did Alice become that in 1375 she was able to lend Walter Fitzwalter £1,000 secured on Egremont Castle. So blatantly avaricious did she grow that in April 1376 'the Good Parliament' petitioned the kind to banish her, and confiscate all her ill-gotten gains. But so long as Edward III remained upon the throne his greedy mistress was safe. After he died in 1377 (whilst Alice purportedly pried the rings from his fingers before rigor mortis set in) her troubles mounted, and for the rest of her life she had to wage a ferocious legal struggle to retain as much of her spoils as she could.

However, Edward IV has an even worse reputation as a womanizer. 'He pursued with no discrimination the married and unmarried, the noble and lowly', wrote an Italian visitor, 'however, he took none by force. He overcame all by money and promises, and having conquered them he dismissed them.'[14] Sir Thomas More did not accept this view, reporting instead that the king had tried to rape the widowed Elizabeth Woodville at knife-point. She vowed to die rather than acceed, and he eventually agreed to marry her. Be that as it may, Edward had three illegitimate children, Arthur, Elizabeth, and Grace, almost certainly all of them by Elizabeth Lucy, a woman from a humble family from the Southampton area. 'He loved her well', wrote the seventeenth-century historian, Sir George Buck, 'and she was his witty concubine, for she was a wanton wench, and willing and ready to yield herself to the king and to his pleasures without conditions.'

Jane Shore was a very different character. Born the daughter of a prosperous London mercer, Thomas Wainstead, she married William Shore, a goldsmith from Lombard Street, whose business frequently took them to court, where she met the king, becoming his mistress in the mid-1470s. By March 1476 she was influential enough for the Pope to commission a group of English bishops to hear her petition for the annulment of her marriage on the grounds of her husband's impotence. There is, however, no record that the action was successful. Sir Thomas More thought her a fine-looking woman. 'Nothing in her body you would have changed, but if you would have wished her somewhat higher', he wrote, adding that she used her considerable influence over Edward entirely for the good, having a ready wit, being merry company, and conducting her affairs with the king, he concluded, so well that his appetites 'did not grieve his people very much'.[15]

One person whom the light-hearted, warm and affectionate mistress upset was the king's younger brother. Soon after Edward IV's death in 1483, Richard III usurped the throne. In the process he probably murdered his young nephews in the Tower, and certainly disgraced Jane Shore. In order to demonstrate his predecessor's degeneracy, and to prove that because Edward IV had never legally married Elizabeth Woodville their children could not inherit the throne, which was now consequently his, Richard III commissioned Friar Ralph Shaw to preach on the text, 'bastard slips shall not take root'.[16] Richard, who was as great a lecher as he was a hypocrite (having sired seven illegitimate children), then accused Jane of witchcraft, before hauling her before the Bishop of London's court as a common harlot. Here she was sentenced to do public penance by walking through the streets of London barefoot, whilst wearing a white sheet, and carrying a lighted taper, and to forfeit all her possessions. According to More she died in London in 1527 'lean, withered and dried up, nothing left but shrivelled skin and bone'.[17] But at least she retained the happy memory of having eighteen years earlier strewn flowers before the funeral procession of Henry VII, the first of the Tudors, who at Bosworth Field in 1485 had destroyed her nemesis, Richard III, thus ending the Middle Ages in England.

III
'NOTHING BUT THE ENGLISH KING'S APPETITE'

When Henry Tudor beat Richard III at the Battle of Bosworth Field on 22 August 1485, and – so Shakespeare would have us believe – plucked the crown from a thorn bush to place it upon his head, few Englishmen thought that he was founding one of the most stable and successful dynasties in their history. For the next hundred and eighteen years the Tudors brought peace to the land, and strengthened the power of the crown and central government.

As the power of the crown increased so too did the importance of the court, the sovereign's intimate household. It was the place where he felt at home, sometimes with his wife and family, at other times with a mistress, and always with friends. The court was a controlled place, in which the monarch could feel at ease. It could be a snug harbour from political storms, or the cockpit where both great issues and petty feuds were resolved. Courtiers, such as the Duke of Norfolk, could also be powerful ministers, who amused Henry VIII whilst he was at home, and fought the king's battles and acted as his ambassador when abroad. Others, such as Henry's fool, Will Somers, were intimates who entertained their master, and if they enjoyed power, did so only because they kept quiet about it. In contrast, men such as Thomas Cromwell exercised their influence from outside the court by trying to use inside intermediaries. Thus they allowed their master to enjoy the pleasure of court life whilst they carried the heavy burden of day-to-day government.

The king had more interesting matters to divert his attention, particularly as the size of the court grew, and attracted exciting people. Although the English court never became the grandiose palace that Louis XIV created at Versailles, as early as the sixteenth century it was the mecca for well-born, ambitious young men and women. By their very nature courts are erotic places, where women wield far more influence than in the male-dominated mundane world outside. To stimulate the interest, and thus the loyalty, of ordinary subjects, courts must be larger-than-life venues of fun, drama and entertainments. Take, for instance, the New Year's Revels staged at Greenwich in 1513. The king and five other courtiers besieged a mock castle which had been built in the hall. Its defenders, six court ladies, 'seeing them so lusty and courageous, were content to solace with them, and upon further communication, to yield the castle, and so they came down and danced a long space'.[1]

Even if the common folk were not allowed entry to witness such festivities, they were often permitted to hang around outside, gaping in deep amazement as the splendid refreshments were carried in, and listening with even greater wonder as the sounds of revelry drifted out. And if, as they walked home to their humdrum lives, they tut-tutted with shocked envy at such goings-on, their fears were often well founded.

Young men and women were – and still are – attracted to centres of power such as courts, in the hope of using their brains and bodies to further their careers. Often they were single: rarely could they bring their families, for wives and children are too dull and restrictive for the glitter of court life. As factions change, the ambitious struggled for the king's ear, for some sign that they are in favour: or else they looked for a new master, as the old one desperately tried to recoup his fortunes.

The linchpin of courtlife was, of course, the sovereign: satisfying his bodily and mental needs was the chief objective of those who served him. For instance, a leading courtier, invariably a knight and member of the Privy Council (no pun intended), was given the great honour of being appointed 'groom of the stool', and was thus required to assist with his majesty's bowel movements. It was the nature of the king's – and to a lesser extent the queen's – libido that determined the sexual climate of the court as a whole. When the king was an uxorious family man court life could be decorous – at least on the surface. If the king was a philanderer, his mistresses might well become the symbols of the various factions which competed for power.

As far as women were concerned Henry Tudor – the seventh King Henry – was a pretty dull fellow. He married Elizabeth,

Edward IV's daughter, for dynastic reasons, in order to link the houses of York and Lancaster. His lack of sexual affairs was due more to a libidinal dearth than any moral surfeit. He considered marrying his eldest son's widow, Catherine of Aragon, to avoid returning her considerable dowry to Spain. As it was he kept Catherine hanging around at court in such humiliating poverty that she complained to her parents, Ferdinand and Isabella, that she had to sell 'bracelets to get a dress of black velvet, for I was all but naked'.[2]

After the sudden death of his eldest son, Arthur, in 1502, Henry Tudor treated his second son, Henry with a similar lack of consideration. He first betrothed the boy to his brother's widow, before breaking off the engagement without consulting either party. The king confined his heir so closely that the Spanish envoy, Guitierre Fuensalida, complained that he 'is locked away like a woman . . . he is so subjugated that he does not speak a word except in response to what the king asks him'.[3] Only once was the boy known to have stood up to his father. When the king toyed with the idea of marrying Joanna, Philip of Castile's widow, who was so mad that she insisted on bringing her late husband in his coffin wherever she went, the prince objected that his father was too old, and she too crazy. Henry Tudor became so angry with his son that it seemed 'as if he sought to kill him', and it was reliably reported that the boy never again said anything in public about affairs of state without his father's permission.

For both the new sovereign and his people the old king's death in 1509 came as a liberation. 'The king is the handsomest prince I ever set eyes upon', one diplomat wrote home.[4] 'His limbs are of gigantic size', wrote another, 'of visage lovely, of body mighty strong'. Among Henry's first acts as king was to marry his brother's widow, Catherine, in obedience, so he later claimed, to his father's dying wish.[5] She made a fine young bride. 'There is nothing wanting in her', concluded Sir Thomas More after seeing Catherine ride through London, 'that the most beautiful girl should have.'[6]

At first the young couple were very happy. Like some perfect knight from the Round Table the king would joust as the queen and her ladies applauded from the side lines. Henry promised his wife that:

4 *Henry VIII*, 'the handsomest prince I ever set eyes upon', by an unknown artist about 1542 (National Portrait Gallery)

As the Holly groweth green
And never changeth hew,
So I am, ever hath been,
Unto my lady true.[7]

The royal couple wrote music together, sang to one another, hunted, hawked, and made love with each other. When Catherine became pregnant it seemed as if their Garden of Eden was complete. Yet almost immediately a worm could be found in their apple.

During his wife's pregnancy custom prevented the king from making love to her, tempting him to seek satisfaction elsewhere. As always there were serpents willing to proffer forbidden fruit. According to Francesco Grimaldi, the Spanish ambassador, Henry made advances to Lady Anne Hastings, the Duke of Buckingham's sister, who had originally been brought to court by her elder sister Elizabeth Fitzwalter, one of Catherine of Aragon's ladies-in-waiting. Soon after marrying George, Lord Hastings, Anne enjoyed a flirtation with Sir William Compton, a groom of the bedchamber, and an intimate of the king's, who may have acted as go-between for Henry and Anne. Anyway, when Elizabeth told George Hastings about his wife's behaviour, he stormed to his wife's bedroom where he found her alone with Compton. Immediately he carried her off to a convent a day's ride away from court. The next morning Buckingham confronted the king about the alleged affair with his sister. The exchange became so heated that Buckingham walked out, vowing never again to spend a night under his majesty's roof. Hearing about the row, Catherine, possibly made more emotional than usual by pregnancy, accused her husband of infidelity. He roundly denied the charge, and retaliated by forcing the queen to dismiss Elizabeth Hastings, an old and dear friend, from her service. 'And the storm continues', the Spanish Ambassador wryly concluded,[8] recognizing that the honeymoon of Henry's fidelity was over almost before it had begun.

Henry's next affair created far less of a rumpus. The queen learned to accept the old Spanish proverb that the light of the sun and the favour of the monarch are not for one alone. The king chose for his bed a low-born foreigner, who was thus neither a threat abroad, nor had powerful relatives at home.[9] Very little is known about Jane Popicourt, who was reputedly the king's mistress in 1514. Probably she was an older, and thus more discreet woman, having first come to England to tutor French to the king's sisters, Mary and Margaret.

Eventually Jane became the mistress of the Duc de Longeville, a French hostage, and developed so promiscuous a reputation that Louis XII refused to accept her back at the French court – in itself quite an achievement.

More is known about the king's next mistress, Elizabeth Blount. She first came to court in 1513 at the age of twelve or thirteen. William, Baron Mountjoy, her kinsman and Henry's close friend, had got her appointed one of the queen's maids of honour. By the end of the following year Elizabeth had matured into such an attractive young woman that one cleric described her as 'eloquent, gracious and beautiful'.[10] She took part in several court festivities. During the Christmas revels she danced with the king so often that Catherine (who was once again heavy with child) persuaded her husband to exclude Elizabeth from the ensuing Twelfth Night masque. But the queen could not control her husband. By 1518 Henry was reported 'in the chains of love with her'. The following spring Elizabeth bore him a son, Henry Fitzroy.

Such a token of his virility delighted the king, particularly because his wife, after several pregnancies, had only been able to produce a daughter, Mary, in 1516. Having done her duty to king, if not country, Henry married Elizabeth off to Sir Gilbert Talboys, a minor courtier, to whom he gave the manor of Rokeby. She remained in rural obscurity for the rest of her life, happily producing six more legitimate children, and remembered by the occasional New Year's present from the king.

As the sovereign's only male offspring, Henry Fitzroy was, of course, far too valuable a being to remain in his mother and step-father's custody: instead he was brought up at court. Among his tutors were Richard Croke, a pioneer of Greek scholarship in England, and John Palsgrave, author of one of the first French Grammars in English. When Henry Fitzroy was six his father created him Duke of Richmond and Surrey, and Lord High Admiral. Within a few years Fitzroy's income from the crown totalled some £4,000 a year. So lavish were the expenditures on the bastard's household that Queen Catherine complained to her husband that it was far larger than that enjoyed by their legitimate child, Mary. This insult to his only son (albeit a bastard one) so angered Henry that he dismissed three of Catherine's Spanish ladies. The Venetian ambassador sardonically noted, 'The Queen was obliged to submit and have patience.'[11]

Perhaps it was the humiliating blatancy of the insult that made

Catherine on this occasion forsake her usual indifference to her husband's affairs. Never once, for instance, had the queen publicly complained about Mary Boleyn.

Mary first entered royal service several years earlier, in May 1514, when she went to France as one of the ladies-in-waiting to Henry VIII's sister, Mary Tudor, who at the age of eighteen married Louis XII. Even though the decrepit fifty-two-year-old French king immediately dismissed most of his young bride's English servants, he retained Mary. After Louis' death the next New Year's Day, Mary, a highly sexed young woman who had been desperate to escape from the boredom of her home at Hever Castle, stayed on in Paris.

The French court was a most erotic place, replete with bawdy books, plays, and accessories. One French prince had a goblet made engraved inside with a picture of a couple making love. He would ask a woman to drain it in a toast, and watch her reaction as the wine unveiled the copulation to see if she were likely to follow suit. Courtiers took pride in their prowess. According to one story, the king's almoner, the cleric Buraud, apologized to a lady for having performed but twelve times during the night: he blamed it all on the medication he was taking.

King Francis I set the tone for his court. It was said that he was 'clothed in women' having three official mistresses as well as dozens of casual liaisons. Years later, much to Henry VIII's chagrin, he described Mary Boleyn as 'a great prostitute, infamous above all'. He claimed that he, like most of his friends, had slept with Mary, who was such a slut that they called her a 'hackney', since like a taxi practically anyone could hire her cheaply for a short run.[12]

In February 1520, soon after her return to England, Mary married William Carey. Through her husband, who as a gentleman of the chamber, was one of the few men allowed access to the king's private rooms, she attracted Henry's attention. Quickly they became intimate, to the apparent satisfaction of all involved. Mary's husband was pliant, her lover was generous, and her father was exceedingly grateful – being rewarded with a stream of sinecures, and the title of Viscount Rochford. The king honoured her by christening one of his ships the *Mary Boleyn* (and not, significantly, the Mary Carey). But when Mary bore him a son in 1525, Henry, as was his habit, sent her back to her husband, who soon afterwards died of the plague.

Two years after the *Mary Boleyn* appeared in the navy list, her sister ship, the *Anne Boleyn* was launched – a clear indication of the king's changing fancy. But this new vessel was not a cockle ready to sail as the king's whims dictated, but rather a battleship, armed by both her elder sister's experience and with her own courage, independence, and determination to resist the heaviest of shells that her sovereign might fire.

The Boleyn family was one of the most ambitious, unscrupulous, pliant, and greediest clans ever to swill at the Tudor trough. Thomas, Mary's father, was descended from a mercer and Lord Mayor of London, while her mother, Elizabeth, was the Earl of Surrey's daughter. Nothing seemed beneath Thomas's ambitions: when it was rumoured that he had introduced both his wife and two daughters into the royal bed to further his career, Henry VIII indignantly retorted, 'Never with the mother'.

It was such unrestrained ambition that prompted Thomas in 1513 to send his youngest and, many said, prettiest daughter, Anne, to be a maid of honour at Margaret of Austria's court, the most fashionable and princely in Europe. On meeting the girl, Margaret wrote to her father, 'I find her so bright and pleasant for her young age'. She was twelve or thirteen at the time, and quickly learned French, and all the requisites of a court lady. She danced gracefully, and became so accomplished a musician that she could play every fashionable composer in the latest style. But perhaps the lesson Anne best learned was the one Margaret taught all her young *protégées* about the fickle blandishments of court life:

> *Trust in those who offer you service*
> *And in the end, my maidens*
> *You will find yourselves in the ranks of those*
> *Who have been deceived.*[13]

In 1515 Anne went to France to join her sister in the service of Mary Tudor, and, after Louis XII died, became lady-in-waiting to Claude, Francis I's long-suffering wife. Here she further honed her courtly abilities, and could have even learned to appreciate art from Leonardo Da Vinci, who had retired to become one of the French queen's pensioners.

In early 1522, as relations between England and France deteriorated, Anne was ordered home, ostensibly to marry James Butler. A couple of months later she made her début at the English court in the Shrove Tuesday Masque, 'The Assault on the Castle of Virtue'.

5 *Anne Boleyn*, executed in 1536. 'She has nothing but the English king's appetite, and her eyes which are black.' Artist unknown (National Portrait Gallery)

This was held in honour of the Imperial Ambassador at York Palace, the London house of Cardinal Wolsey, the king's chief minister. Anne was one of eight ladies who, dressed in white satin with Milanese headdresses expensively decorated with Venetian gold, represented female virtues. They guarded the battlements of a mock castle, under which eight choristers dressed as Indians sang and marched sentry duty. After Desire, accoutred in crimson, tried in vain to persuade the ladies to leave their ramparts, eight masked gentlemen entered to the salute of cannons. With dates, oranges, and other fruits they pelted the defenders, who responded by pouring down rose water (which was much more romantic, and far safer than the traditional boiling oil). After several minutes of mock combat, the ladies surrendered. They descended to the floor to dance with the gallants, who took off their masks to reveal themselves as high-born courtiers, led by none other than the king.

To modern ears all this sounds ridiculous nonsense. But at the time it was the very essence of court life, in which honour was valued far more than cold economic calculations, and where serving the king counted above all else. In retrospect, too, the masque was uncannily prophetic. Over the next decade Henry spent much time persuading Anne to come down from the battlements, while she – having been cast in the masque as Perseverance – resisted heroically.

Soon after the Shrove Tuesday celebrations Anne fell in love with Percy, the Earl of Northumberland's son, who was living in Cardinal Wolsey's household. Even though he returned her affection, both families objected: Percy was betrothed to Mary Talbot, the Earl of Shrewsbury's daughter, while the Boleyns still hoped to marry Anne to James Butler. When Henry heard about the infatuation he was 'much offended' and ordered Wolsey to stop it. 'I marvel not a little at thy peevish folly', the cardinal reprimanded Percy, 'that thou wouldest tangle, and insure thyself with a foolish girl.'[14] Percy's defence of Anne as but 'a simple maid', made not the slightest difference: his father forced him into a brief, but very unhappy marriage with Mary Talbot.

It would be tempting to assume that Anne's hatred of Wolsey sprang from the cardinal's castigation of her lover, and that the king ordered the affair ended to reserve 'the simple maid' for himself. But such implies far too much hindsight: Henry's own marriage to Catherine had not yet broken down, and anyway Anne was still too inexperienced to interest the king.

As punishment for her foolishness with Percy, Anne was briefly exiled from court. On her return she became involved with Thomas Wyatt, the outstanding poet of his generation, who was born in Kent, about twenty miles from the Boleyn's seat at Hever. Given as much to women as he was to understatement, Wyatt once confessed, 'I grant I do not profess chastity'. Unhappily married in his youth to that frigid female, Elizabeth Brooke, Thomas knew that he was an exceptionally good looking blade:

> *Nature made Wyatt tall with powerful muscles*
> *And sinews strong, adding thereunto a face,*
> *As beautiful as any.*

So thought Wyatt's friend, John Leland. Later historians have used Wyatt's own verse as evidence that Anne surrendered to his charms completely.

> *A love rewarded with disdain,*
> *Yet it is love. What will you more?*

asked the poet, claiming that his mistress was 'wild to hold'.[15] But Wyatt might have been referring to some woman other than Anne, and even if he had been, he could well have been doing so in the exaggerated language of courtly love. If his love had been requited, and if he and Anne had been intimate, surely their affair could not have stayed secret for long amid the gossip-ridden milieu of Henry's court? Could Wyatt have survived the purge of all those remotely suspected of having been Queen Anne's lovers?

During the mid-1520s Henry's life and reign reached a turning point. He realized that he had not succeeded in fulfilling 'his ambition not merely to equal, but to excel the glorious deeds of his ancestors' by conquering France. His first marriage had also failed.[16] Once he had loved Catherine as 'my most dear and well beloved consort'.[17] Now he hated her as his brother's barren widow, who obstinately stood between him and the siring of a son. If England were to be spared the horrors of civil war it must have a male heir.

Henry stopped sleeping with his wife in 1524. She was thirty-nine, and since her last conception had been seven years earlier, it was obvious she could not give him a son. So in May 1527 the king secretly started proceedings for a divorce.

It was at about this time Henry first noticed Anne Boleyn, whose wit and independence contrasted with his wife's papist piety and sanctimonious devotion. Although Anne was 'not one of the handsomest women in the world', being, for instance, far less attractive than Bessie Blount, most around the king recognized her allures. Quite simply, Anne radiated sex appeal. 'She is of middling stature, swarthy complexion, long neck, wide mouth, a bosom not much raised', wrote a Venetian diplomat with a delicacy that did credit to his profession. He concluded that she 'in fact has nothing but the English king's appetite, and her eyes which are black'.[18]

With Henry's appetite on her side no woman needed more. Anne seemed to rejuvenate the king, a man entering middle age, of marginal potency, who desperately needed a male heir, and who was tormented by deep-seated fears of his own sexual inadequacies. When the Imperial Ambassador hinted that taking a younger wife might not necessarily produce the longed-for son, Henry indignantly asked, 'Am I not a man like other men? Am I not? Am I not?'[19]

But Anne was a woman unlike any he had ever before pursued. While she enjoyed being the king's mistress in the play-world of unrequited love, in the real one of the flesh she refused to become his lover. Henry's love-letters show that after a year of courtly games he had become so enthralled that 'if it please you . . . to give yourself body and soul to me', the king promised 'to take you as my sole mistress, casting off all others'.[20] And if she refused, Henry sighed, 'I could do none other than lament me of my ill fortune, abetting by little and little my so great folly.' The king's great folly replied by sending him a trinket portraying a woman safely aboard ship, secure from all storms. Thus she made it perfectly clear that only as his wife would she share his bed.

Anne was, however, prepared to allow him partial privileges. 'God that I would you were in my arms or I in yours, for I think that it long since I kissed you', penned the king in one love-letter. In another, he wrote 'wishing myself (especially of an evening) in my sweetheart's arms, whose pretty duckies [breasts] I trust shortly to kiss'.[21]

A public demonstration of Anne's private powers over Henry came in the summer of 1528. It involved the appointment of a new abbess of Wilton following the death of Cecily de Willoughby in April. Wilton was a rather genteel nunnery, the sort of place to which unmarried daughters or surplus widows could be consigned without forcing them to endure a regime of excessive religious rigour. Wolsey told the nuns to elect Isabel Jordayn as their abbess, but Anne prevailed on Henry to support Mary Carey's sister-in-law,

Eleanor. When someone told the king that Eleanor was utterly unsuitable, having had two bastards by a priest, and someone else let him know that Isabel was nearly as bad, having had several lovers, Henry nominated a third person. Due to a failure of communications, and the cardinal's dismissal of Anne as a mere woman, and thus of no consequence, the nuns went ahead and elected his nominee. Outraged, Henry subjected Wolsey to one of his notorious tantrums.

Having broken with the cardinal, Anne and the Boleyns emerged as a separate faction, determined on revenge. They used the failure of Wolsey's foreign policy to destroy him. Already annoyed at Wolsey for allowing the Holy Roman Emperor, Charles V, and Francis I to make peace behind England's back by signing the Treaty of Cambrai, the king was even more frustrated by the cardinal's inability to obtain a divorce.

In normal times persuading the pope to annul a king's marriage, and stigmatize a queen of two decades as a whore whom he had lived with in sin, would have presented few obstacles. But the sack of Rome by troops theoretically owing allegiance to Charles V (Anne's nephew) meant for Pope Clement VII that times were far from normal. A virtual prisoner, the Holy Father had to stall. When Henry VIII demanded the case come to trial in England, Clement VII sent Cardinal Campeggio to London with secret instructions to string things out for as long as possible. After procrastinating for nine months, Campeggio, sitting with Wolsey, opened proceedings in May 1529. But in July he adjourned hearings until October to observe the long summer holiday the Vatican took to escape Rome's unbearable heat. Outraged by this transparent ploy, the Duke of Suffolk 'gave a great clap on the table with his hand', and shouted out 'By the mass, now I see the old said saw is true, that there was never legate or cardinal that did good in England.'[22]

Anne did all she could to ensure that Cardinal Wolsey did not stay in power for long. According to one story she told the king that if anyone else had treated him half as badly as Wolsey, they should 'have lost their heads'. Certainly the Cardinal was mortally afraid of Anne's anger. 'If you love my life', he told his factotum, Thomas Cromwell, 'all possible means must be used for attaining her favour.'[23] But the time for winning Lady Anne's favour had long since passed. In October 1529 Henry dismissed Wolsey. A year later he died at St Mary's Abbey, Leicester, a broken man, on his way to the Tower of London and certain execution.

The disgrace of the minister who had dominated English affairs for two decades left a profound vacuum that Anne and her faction tried to fill by forming an alliance with Thomas Cromwell. Both encouraged the king to listen to the arguments of religious reformers, such as William Tyndale, that as a sovereign he did not need the pope's permission to put away his wife. But at first Henry shrank from such a step: it was not only a revolution that undid a millennium of obedience to Rome, but it could condemn the king to eternal damnation. Henry wavered. England drifted. The Boleyns faded. And so in one last desperate throw Anne placated the king's fears about his soul by playing her one and only ace – her body.

Speculation about their physical relationship had been rife for years. As long ago as 1527 it had been rumoured that they were sleeping together. In June 1529 the French ambassador reported, 'I much fear that for some time past the king has come very close to Mademoiselle Anne.'[24] Others have suggested that it was only after Henry banished his wife from court in the summer of 1531 that the two became intimate. On 1 September 1532 Henry made Anne Marchioness of Pembroke in her own right (with the title to succeed to all her children, even those not lawfully begotten) and gave her lands worth £1,000 a year. Whether the king's generosity was a reward for services already bestowed, or a down payment for favours due, is a matter for conjecture. We know that during a trip they made to Calais the following month they lodged in adjoining rooms, with a connecting door, and that in the middle of December Anne conceived a child. Absolutely sure that it would be a son, Henry secretly married his mistress on about 25 January 1533, so as to legitimize the boy, and ensure the succession.

The rest of the story is well known. Henry's second wife had a child, a daughter, Elizabeth – much to the king's disappointment, although greatly to the kingdom's benefit. Henry broke with Rome, and established the Church of England, while Cromwell changed the nature of government so drastically that some have called it a revolution. Anne and Henry tried to have other children, but none survived. Henry, whose ability to love was as fickle and fierce as his capacity for hate, had Mistress Anne beheaded on Tower Green in 1536. A day later he married that chaste mouse, Jane Seymour. Anne's reign as queen had been one of a thousand days: her tenure as the king's mistress was even briefer. Yet no other mistress more affected England's history.

After loving Anne the king never again loved as intensely. To be sure there were stories about a royal dalliance. Queen Anne attributed a miscarriage to her husband's involvement with 'another very beautiful maid', perhaps Anne Shelton. Honor Lisle, the ambitious wife of the egregious royal governor of Calais, schemed to get her daughter, Anne Basset, into the royal bed. But Henry seemed to have tired of extramarital affairs. He appeared to wallow in canards about Anne's infidelities, boasting that she must have slept with more than a hundred men. 'You never saw a Prince, not man', noted the Imperial Ambassador, 'who made greater show of his horns.'[25]

Anne had soured the cuckold king of illicit love, and after her death he looked for happiness within marriage. He had a son by Jane Seymour, who died in childbirth. Then he claimed he could not consummate his fourth marriage with Anne of Cleves, the Flanders Mare being too repulsive. His fifth wife, the young and promiscuous Katherine Howard, made a laughing stock of her middle-aged husband and like Anne paid for her folly with her life. With his sixth, the piously Protestant widow, Catherine Parr, Henry enjoyed some happiness in his old age, his philandering days long since past.

Mistresses played little part in the lives of Henry's successors. Edward VI died at the age of fifteen, too young for the priggish lad to have indulged in anything very much. Queens Mary I and Elizabeth I were subject to the sexual double standard that females trespassed at their direst peril.

The reign of Mary Queen of Scots dramatically demonstrated the dangers of flaunting the double standard. About ten days after she was born in early December 1542 Mary's father, James V of Scotland, died – apparently from despair at having heard that the English had thrashed his army at the Battle of Solway Moss. When Mary was six her mother, the Regent of Scotland, betrothed her to Francis, the French Dauphin, and sent her to be brought up in Paris. Ten years later, in 1558, she married the sickly heir, and became Queen of France in 1560 when her husband inherited following the death of his father, Henry II. But Francis II died the following year, leaving Mary a childless widow of eighteen, who promptly returned to her native land, to rule as queen in her own right.

Impervious to sage advice, and oblivious to the reformation that John Knox had engendered in Scotland's church and morals, Mary married Henry Stewart, Lord Darnley with an indecent haste. At first she found his good looks – which were exceeded only by his arrogance – irresistible, calling him 'the properest and best proportioned long man she had ever seen'.[26]

The marriage broke down soon after their first child was conceived and they parted. Convinced that Mary was having an affair with David Rizzio, her Italian secretary, Darnley had him savagely stabbed to death, almost in front of the queen, who was six months pregnant. When her husband fell ill, perhaps from smallpox, or else from syphilis (which would explain his insane jealousy), Mary pretended to forgive him, whilst all the time plotting with the Earl of Bothwell. As a result Darnley was murdered in most suspicious circumstances at the Kirk of the Fields just outside Edinburgh. If any of Mary's subjects had doubts about the queen's relations with Bothwell before Darnley's death, few had afterwards. Convinced that she had become mistress of this squat man, whom a contemporary historian described as 'an ape in purple',[27] many of the Scots nobility raised an army. Notwithstanding her belated marriage, they forced Mary into exile in England, where she was eventually executed for plotting against Elizabeth I. They drove Bothwell to Denmark. After being purportedly chained to a pillar half his height so he could never stand upright, the wretched man died insane at Dragsholm, where the curious can still inspect his mummified corpse.

Both paid a terrible price for flaunting the double standard. But at least Mary died bravely. She left a son who not only inherited the thrones of England and Scotland, but whose reign demonstrated that homosexual affairs could be even more damaging than heterosexual ones.

IV

'NEITHER GOD, NOR ANGEL, BUT A MAN LIKE ANY OTHER'

Over the years no British monarch has been portrayed as a bigger buffoon than James VI of Scotland and I of England. He was called 'the Wisest Fool in Christendom', and 'God's silly vassal'. On being advised that he should leave court more often to show himself to his people throughout the country so as to win their loyalty, James asked with characteristic vulgarity if he was expected 'to pull down my breeches and they shall also see my arse?' During the king's lifetime Sir Anthony Weldon (a biased source, who was as scathing as he was unreliable) described him as a bandy-legged clown, constantly slobbering as drink dribbled out of his ill-fitting mouth, dripping down a straggly beard to stain a dirty padded waistcoat, 'his eyes ever rowling after any stranger . . . his fingers . . . ever fiddling about his codpiece'.[1]

Posterity has agreed with this piquantly delicious malice. The eminent Victorian historian, Thomas Babington Macaulay, described James as 'stammering, slobbering, shedding unmanly tears, trembling at a drawn sword, and talking alternately in the style of a buffoon and a pedagogue'.[2]

One most important reason for the hostility of contemporaries as well as later historians towards James was his fondness for attractive young men. According to Weldon when James said goodbye to one of his favourites, Robert Carr, the Earl of Somerset, 'he kissed him about his neck, slabbering his cheeks saying, "when shall I see you again? Oh My soul I shall neither eat nor sleep until I see you again" '.[3] Sometimes the king's declarations of love for his favourites became so excessive that they could be described as blasphemy, mitigated by unconscious irony. 'I, James, am neither God nor angel, but a man like any other', he once told the privy council about his feelings towards George Villiers, Duke of Buckingham, adding, 'Jesus Christ did the same and therefore I cannot be blamed. Christ had his John and I have my George.' James nicknamed his George 'Steenie', after St Stephen, because he too had a face that the Bible compared to that 'of an angel'.[4]

All too often James became mawkish. 'I care for match nor nothing, so I may once have you in my arms again', he wrote to Buckingham, 'God grant it! God grant it! God grant it! Amen, amen, amen.'[5] A year later, like an ageing husband trying to recapture the passion he had enjoyed long ago during his honeymoon with a younger spouse, James wrote to his favourite that 'we may make at this Christmas a new marriage, ever to be kept'.[6]

Apart from being the most important influence in his personal life, James's extra-marital relations affected his reign as King of Great Britain in three significant ways. His first affair, with Esmé Stuart, Duke of Lennox, made him an even more canny person, determined to be master of Scotland. His second liaison, with Robert Carr, ended in a nasty scandal which helped widen the gulf between court and county. During the reign of his son this gap became a fatally wide chasm into which Charles I eagerly tumbled. James's third ménage, with George Villiers, permitted an ambitious favourite to monopolize royal power with disastrous consequences.

Because Charles's problems lay a long time in the future, recently several historians have astutely observed that there was no high road between James's peccadillos and his son's failed policies. If James is not taken at face value, if what he achieved, rather than the nonsense he babbled with saccharin affection is taken into account, then the king's record is impressive. The dirty old monarch who would scratch his private parts, and lean upon a favourite's shoulders during diplomatic audiences, also presided over the translation of the Bible, the peak of Shakespeare's dramatic performances, the unification of England and Scotland, the plantation of Ulster, and the foundation of the British Empire.

It is no accident that the recent revival of James's historical reputation has occurred during a time of growing toleration of homosexuality. Just as today many gays have emerged from the closet, so historians have started to examine monarchs more openly. We should not be surprised when they tell us that out of the thirty-two adult kings of England since the Norman Conquest two (or 6.4 per cent), Edward II and James I, were predominantly homosexual, and that three more (or 9.6 per cent), William II,

Richard I and William III, were purportedly so inclined. In 1948 the *Kinsey Report* noted that of adult white American males 8 per cent were exclusively homosexual while 37 per cent admitted to having an orgasm with other men.[7]

It is none the less an indication of the continuing double standard that has been drawn between sexual relations with persons of the opposite sex and those of the same, that the English language has no word which applies to them both. Until 1967 in Britain all homosexual relations have been illicit, for both law and society have sanctified only unions between men and women. The cruel epithets used to describe homosexuals (which come so readily to mind that they need no repetition) even after the legalization of such behaviour between consenting adults, are a linguistic indication of the hostility the sexual majority still feels towards the minority.[8]

During the seventeenth century many courtiers reacted vehemently to James's advances. A contemporary reported that the Earl of Holland spurned them 'by turning aside, and spitting after the king had slabbered in his mouth'.[9] But most Jacobean politicians came to accept the king's preferences – they had no alternative if they wanted to remain in politics. Some even tried to inveigle new young men into the royal bed to be used as playthings for his majesty's fancies and conduits for their own ambitions. Although young women have, of course, from time immemorial been used in a similar fashion, the results with males were very different. Women, be they wives or mistresses were supposed to remain subservient. But male lovers were permitted, even expected to exercise power. Unlike James I, Elizabeth I realized that inviting a man into the royal bed posed grave political dangers for an ageing queen. Indeed, as her infatuation with the headstrong Earl of Essex (who was executed in 1601 for trying to overthrow the government) showed, an alliance with a spoilt young favourite was replete with pitfalls even without a physical basis.

King James's sexual preferences may be traced back to his birth and childhood. He was the only son of Mary Queen of Scots and Henry Stewart, Lord Darnley, being born on 19 June 1566, months after his parent's marriage had collapsed. Darnley, as will be recalled, became insanely jealous of his wife's apparently platonic friendship with her Italian secretary, David Rizzio, whom he had stilettoed to death, almost before her eyes. It has been suggested that this prenatal trauma rendered James pathologically afraid of unsheathed knives and assassination attempts. Mary roundly denied her husband's suspicions of having been intimate with Rizzio, saying, as she presented their four-hour-old baby to him. 'My Lord, God has given you and me a son, begotten by none but you.'[10] Such pronouncements did nothing to assuage James's concerns about his paternity. As an adult the quip that he should be called 'Britain's Solomon' – a title that the pedagogue in James usually relished – because he really was the son of David reduced him to a paroxysm of tears.

Outraged by both Mary's part in her husband's murder, and her promiscuity with the Earl of Bothwell, the Scots forced the queen to abdicate in favour of her thirteen-month-old son. Since James had never known his mother he was not close to her. He did not enquire after her health whilst she was a prisoner in England, neither did he express much grief on learning of her execution.

The lack of a surrogate mother harmed James's childhood development as much, if not more, than the absence of a real one. For the first three years of his reign his uncle, the Earl of Moray, ruled Scotland as regent. When he was assassinated in 1570, James's grandfather, the Earl of Lennox took over the regency for a couple of years, until Mary's supporters shot him in the back during a coup attempt. James never forgot seeing his dying grandfather being carried into Stirling Castle. The king's next governor, the Earl of Mar and his wife, were very strict with the five-year-old boy. So too was his chief tutor, the ferociously Calvinistic pedant, George Buchannan, who constantly reminded the lad of his mother's wickedness, and her son's sins. 'As a king he exists only for his subjects', taught this twisted misogynist, 'his life must be the pattern for every citizen.'[11]

In theory, at least, James accepted such pious pronouncements, uttering during his adulthood more than enough platitudes of his own. Once he advised his eldest son to be 'of good fame, and without blemish, otherwise what will people think'.[12] He instructed his chief minister that sodomy be one of the three crimes exempted from a general pardon. But the canyon between what the king practised and what he preached was so grand that harsh critics have dismissed him as a hypocrite, while more charitable ones have written him off as the most ridiculous neurotic ever to sit on the British throne.

James's education was long and hard, with hardly a moment's rest. 'Thay gar me speik Latin ar I could speik Scottis', he later complained about being forced to use Latin before he knew his native tongue.[13] Even though he became a scholar of note, who once admitted that had he not been born a prince he would have loved to be an Oxford don, his education left him deeply anxious and desperate for affection – a not unusual combination, even amongst professors.[14] As an old man he started to tremble when he espied a courtier who reminded him of Buchannan. As a young king he confessed to his people that he had grown up 'alone, without father or mother, brother or sister'.[15]

Perhaps James was recalling 15 September 1579, the day a lonely, insecure thirteen-year-old monarch, desperate for affection, first met his cousin, Esmé Stuart. It was a case of love at first sight, for a fortnight later the two were reported riding together for Edinburgh. They were an odd couple – the bandy-legged ugly royal duckling, pawky with his uncouth Scots ways; and the handsomely self-confident swan, three or four years James's senior. Just home from an expensive education in Paris, Esmé exuded Gallic glamour. All agreed that he was as good looking as he was charming. He was blessed with red hair, and a striking auburn beard that enhanced his unusually dark eyes. His aristocratic face had high cheekbones, and a straight nose. His fine healthy body attracted the king, who always felt ashamed of his own weedy limbs.

James made no secret of his love. 'At this time His Majesty, having conceived an invaird affection', wrote David Moyie, Clerk of the Privy Council, 'entered with great familiarities and quiet purposed with him.' Another contemporary observed that James was 'in such love with him as in the open sight of the people, oftentimes he will clasp him about the neck with his arms and kiss him'.[16] The ministers of the kirk were, quite understandably, outraged, complaining that this new paramour had 'corrupted', and 'abused' the king. Andrew Melville, head of the Presbyterian General Assembly, declared that Esmé held James 'in a misty night of captivity and black darkness of servitude'.[17]

But – as was so often the case – politics rather than morality proved to be the favourite's undoing. Esmé's rise in royal favour, and thus political power, was rocket-like: the fuse was lit, and amidst a cascade of sparks Esmé soared to the heights, exploding in a shower of stars, that became no more than a burnt stick which tumbled to the ground leaving behind but the faint whiff of burnt gunpowder.

Within a month of their first meeting James publicly revealed his infatuation by announcing that he intended to create Esmé the Earl of Lennox. Soon afterward he gave his new friend the rich Abbey of Arbroath. The pledge seemed to be no more than a down-payment for the earnest of the king's love. But the nobility feared that James intended mortgaging Scotland. The following year he gave Esmé the Barony of Torbolton, lands in Crooktown and Renfrewshire, and made him Lord Chancellor and First Gentleman of the Bed Chamber.

All along Esmé was playing for higher stakes than mere money and titles. The Guises had originally sent him back to Scotland to restore French and Catholic influence there. Esmé had not been home for eight days when he took full advantage of his first meeting with the king at Stirling to do so. Once James's affection was secure, with much publicity and scant sincerity the favourite renounced his Catholic faith so as to win the support of the moderate Calvinist nobles. With the help of Captain James Stewart of Bothwellmuir, he also set out to destroy James Douglas, Earl of Morton, and leader of the ultra-Protestant faction. Esmé dragged Douglas before the privy council and charged him with the murder of the king's little-lamented father, Darnley. The earl was convicted and publicly executed in Edinburgh.

Esmé's triumph, exacerbated by a severe attack of hubris (for at this time he was also plotting to invade England at the head of a Spanish army), produced the inevitable reaction, known as the Raid of Ruthven. On 22 August 1582 the Earl of Gowrie took advantage of a rare separation of James and Esmé to stage a *coup d'état*. Meeting the king, who was out hunting near Perth, he invited him back to enjoy the hospitality of his nearby castle at Ruthven. The following morning, when James tried to leave, he found the gates barred. Brutally, Gowrie forced the tearful lad to dismiss his friend, sending him back to France. Here, a couple of years later Esmé died, a miserable exile, whose last request was for his heart be embalmed and returned to James – the only person to whom it had ever been given.[18]

The trauma of the Raid of Ruthven – which was but one more incident in the long brutal history of Caledonian clan feuds – affected the king profoundly. For James it had been more of a rape than a raid. Humiliated he burst into tears, only to be gruffly scolded by one of his captors, the Master of Glamis, 'Better that bairns should weep than bearded men.' James never forgot the insult. Years later he complained about the 'feckless arrogant conceit of their greatness and power'.[19] The affront to James as a monarch goaded him into making the most grandiose claims about the divine right of kings. At the same time the intensity of his first love reinforced his sexual preferences. Broken-hearted the king asked:

> *And shall I like a bird or beast forget*
> *For any storms that threatening heaven can send*
> *The object sweet, where'on my heart is set*
> *For whom to serve all my senses, all I bend?*

Even though women had nothing to do with Esmé's fall, illogically the experience made James more of a misogynist. 'Even so all women are of nature vain', he wrote a few months later, 'and cannot keep no secret unrevealed.' Esmé's dismissal was a savage lesson in the advantages of keeping one's own council. It made the king even more canny and Machiavellian in his dealings. He wrote:

> *Since thought is free, think what you will*
> *O troubled heart to ease thy pain*
> *Though unrevealed can do no ill*
> *But world put out turn not a gain.*
> *Be careful, aye, for to invent*
> *The way to get thine own intent . . .*
> *With patience then to see thou attend*
> *And hope to vanquish at the end.*[20]

And long before the end the king certainly vanquished his enemies. He destroyed the power of the old Scottish nobles and increased that of the crown so effectively that he could truly boast that he governed his native land by the mere stroke of a pen. Thus James has been called 'the most successful King of Scotland since Robert Bruce'.[21]

When the Gowrie family tried to repeat their coup on 5 August 1600, James showed how well he had learned from the Raid on Ruthven. Once again whilst out hunting he unexpectedly met the Earl of Gowrie's younger brother, the Master of Ruthven, who invited the royal party back to the hospitality of their house near

Perth. Following an impromptu dinner the king retired alone with the master to a turret room, from which soon were heard frantic cries of 'Treason! Treason!' Suspecting the worst, the king's servants rushed to rescue their master, slaughtering the two Gowrie brothers in the process. The story of what actually happened is murky. According to the king (who was never conscious of the humour of his explanations) the Master of Ruthven invited him to the turret room to see a pot of gold, and then locked the door and pulled a dagger which he held to his heart. Many accepted James's explanation that he was the innocent victim of another kidnap attempt; the queen (who knew better than most about these things) did not, being convinced that it was all part of a botched homosexual encounter.[22]

James recognized that if he wanted to maintain the powers he had won for the Scots monarchy, as well as inherit the English throne, he must (as he explained to the privy council) have an heir, and thus needed to take a wife. With a straight face the king professed that he was not marrying for carnal reasons: 'as to my own nature, God is my witness, I could have abstained longer,' he told the councillors, none of whom had cause to doubt his sincerity.[23]

Of the various brides who were suggested, James chose the youngest, Anne, the Danish king's daughter. She was a stereotypical nordic beauty – tall, statuesque, with snow-white skin and golden flowing hair. She had a full body and a slight mind. Excited by reports of her physical allures, and disappointed when a storm forced the ship bringing her to Scotland back to Norway, James brushed aside diplomatic protocol to sail personally to Oslo to collect his bride. Apart from the deaths from pneumonia of two Africans who had been especially commissioned to dance in snow, the wedding celebrations of August 1589 were a great success. Anne's return to Edinburgh the following May, in a silver chariot drawn by eight horses, was an even grander triumph. James revelled in his new-found heterosexual bliss, telling his wife:

> *As on the wings of your enchanting fame*
> *I was transported ou'r the stormied sea.*[24]

The happy couple quickly had a child, a son, whom they christened Henry, perhaps to flatter Queen Elizabeth or else to strengthen the infant's claim to the English throne. But the fruit of their joy proved to be its cancered undoing. When James insisted that the Earl of Mar, the traditional guardian of the Scots heir, bring up the baby,

6 *Anne of Denmark, wife of James I*, in masque costume. Miniature by Isaac Oliver dated about 1610 (By gracious permission of Her Majesty The Queen)

Anne vehemently protested against being separated from her child. In the short term the king won: but in the long run, even though he and Anne had six more children, James lost the love of his wife.

Initially, however, the king did not return to other men for solace. There is some evidence that during the 1590s he had an affair with Anne Murray of Tallbardine, who was married to Patrick Lyon, Lord Glamis. A diplomat described her as 'the king's mistress',[25] while James, with his characteristic sense of discretion wrote a poem, 'A Dream on his mistress, my Ladie Glammes', in which he described how 'the god Morpheus brought Anne to his bed whilst he was sleeping'.

By the time Queen Elizabeth died in 1603 and James succeeded to the throne of what he called 'the promised land' of England, his interest in women was dormant enough to allow his new subjects to snigger at the Latin tag, 'Rex fuit Elizabeth, nunc est regina Jacobus.'[26] He may possibly have had a brief fling with James Hay, a Scottish favourite, whom he rewarded with English riches and titles, including the viscountcy of Doncaster. More certainly, in 1606, the day after the birth of their last child, Sophia, he ceased sleeping with his wife. Worn out, and doubtless relieved, the queen retired to seek solace in Catholic piety, and her hunting dogs, as the king returned to the comforts of pretty young men.

Paramount amongst his paramours was Robert Carr, a young Scots lad, whose looks greatly exceeded both his modesty and intelligence. In 1603 Carr had been a pageboy who ran alongside the royal coach during James's triumphant ride south from Edinburgh to claim the English throne. James never appeared to notice the runner, who on arriving in London was discharged from his service.

Carr travelled for some time in France, before returning to court in 1607. Soon afterwards he attracted the king's attention when he fell and broke his leg during a joust. James visited the patient, supervising his nurses, doctors, and diet, while trying to teach the lad some Latin. Even though he learned little Latin (the London wags suggested that the inarticulate Scots youth be taught English instead), by the time his leg was mended he was well and truly the king's favourite. 'The Prince leaneth on his arm, pinches his cheek, smooths his ruffled garment [and] doth much covet his presence', wrote an observer, adding that 'this fellow is straight limbed, well favoured, strong shouldered and smooth faced'.[27] Carr's rise was rapid. On 23 December James knighted him, and the following March made him Viscount Rochester. The next year James gave the stripling the privy council seat vacated by the elder statesman, Sir Robert Cecil, and in 1612 created him Earl of Somerset.

There seemed no favour beyond the favourite's asking. When Carr fell in love with Frances Howard, the Earl of Essex's wife, the king bullied the bishops into annulling her marriage because it had not been consummated by her impotent husband, a charge the Earl vehemently denied. Most people refused to accept the findings of a panel of matrons, who examined her ladyship, hidden under a cloud of veils to spare her modesty, that she was still virgo intacto. Instead they believed that a genuine virgin had been smuggled in her lady-ship's stead.[28] Oblivious to such canards James, like a proud father of the bride, paid for the Carr's sumptuous wedding on Boxing Day 1613, and even sold lands worth £10,000 to give Frances a dowry fit for the wife of a royal paramour.

Surprisingly James never minded when those he loved married. In fact he was pruriently interested in the most intimate details of their conjugal lives, and adopted their progeny as if they were his own grandchildren. Carr's undoing was not taking another to his bed, but taking himself too seriously. 'You may lead me by the heart and not by the nose', James warned him, but 'If I ever find that you think to retain me by one sparkle of fear, all the violence of my love will in that instant be changed into as violent a hatred.'[29]

Frances Carr vehemently loathed Sir Thomas Overbury, her husband's friend and adviser, for opposing their marriage. To get him out of the way she had the king offer him an ambassadorship to Russia. When he impertinently turned it down, he was imprisoned in the Tower of London, where she secretly poisoned him – the romantics say with tarts baked by Her Ladyship's own fair hand, the prosaic with an enema of mercury.

Anyway, two years after Overbury died, apparently one more victim of England's most feared prison, an apothecary's apprentice confessed from what he assumed was his death bed in Antwerp that whilst in London he had supplied the Carrs with poison. Eventually they were brought to trial, during which James stationed two Yeomen of the Guard with large cloaks beside Robert to muffle him in case he blurted out the most intimate details of their relationship. The Carrs were condemned to death, and although (unlike their accomplices, including the garrulous apprentice) they were not executed, their time in the royal favour was over.

So the whole sordid scandal did the crown immense harm. Compared to Elizabeth's court, which emphasized platonic love and the cult of Virginiana, James's was a moral morass that offended many of his increasingly puritan subjects. They described his love affairs as 'prostitution'. They were horrified by the bacchanalia which occurred in 1605 when the king created Charles, his second son, Duke of York. Anne and several of her ladies performed in a masque painted up as blackamoors, and wearing costumes that exposed so much of their breasts that even jaded courtiers were shocked. The revelations were not, however, sufficiently stimulating to explain the feeding frenzy which took place after the dramatic presentation. As flunkies carried in a sumptuous banquet the audience charged, collapsing the tables and sending the delicacies flying, to be trampled underfoot. Sober citizens found the behaviour at the masque the following year for Anne's brother, Christian IV of Denmark, even more outrageous. Everyone – from their majesties down – got beastly drunk, including the ladies playing Faith, Hope, and Charity, who had to be led off stage too 'sick and spewing' to say their lines.[30]

Many plain folk found murder, adultery, and sodomy – the key ingredients that the Carrs brought to the Overbury affair – as financially ruinous as they were morally disgusting. 'The setting up of these golden calves cost England more than Queen Elizabeth spent in all her wars', complained one contemporary. 'The kingdom', concluded Archbishop Abbot, 'was glad to be rid of Carr.'[31]

Most politicians, however, whose ambitions had long since dulled their scruples, welcomed Carr's ruin as an opportunity for personal advantage. Even Archbishop Abbot was not above a little pandering – albeit in a good cause. To try to shift royal policy in a more protestant direction, he dangled a new young man before the old king. Like most pimps, His Grace of Canterbury stressed the bodily attractions of George Villiers, the paramour for whom he was trying to solicit: 'he had a very lovely complexion, he was the handsomest bodied man in England, his limbs were so well compacted.'

George was born in 1592, the second son of a second marriage of Leicestershire gentry of the second rank. His mother sent her good-looking and exceedingly charming boy to France, where he learned the sophisticated arts of riding, dancing, fencing, and conversation that James had found so appealing in both Esmé Stuart and Robert Carr. The king first met the man who was to sign himself 'Your majesty's slave and dog', as he dominated the last few years of his reign, in a particularly appropriate venue – the kennels of Apethorpe House, Northamptonshire. They first became intimate in August

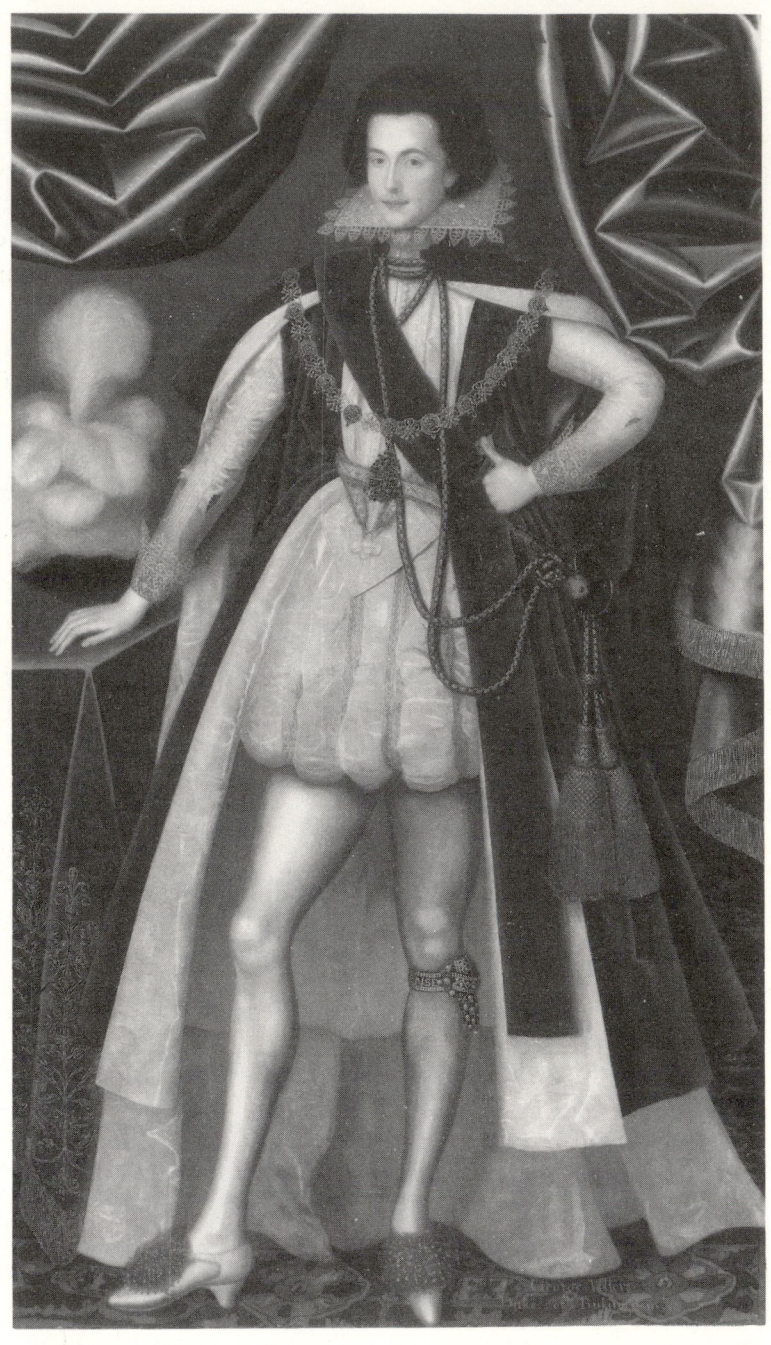

7 *George Villiers, first Duke of Buckingham*, 'the handsomest bodied man in England'. Portrait attributed to William Larkin, about 1616 (National Portrait Gallery)

1615 at Farnham where, as Villiers recalled, 'the bed's head could not be found between the master and his dog'.[32]

George's rise in royal favour 'was so quick that it seemed rather a flight than a growth'. The king made him Master of the Horse and a Viscount in 1615, Master of the Wardrobe and Earl of Buckingham in 1616, a marquis in 1618, and ultimately a duke in 1623. 'No man danced, no man runs or jumps better', a contemporary sourly noted about Buckingham, 'indeed he jumped higher than any Englishmen did in so short a time from private gentleman to dukedom'.[33]

Many assumed that Buckingham was yet one more lover in a long line, whom James would discard when another, more attractive paramour came along. Thus they used the traditional ploy of trawling younger bedmates in front of the king in the hope of changing his policies. In 1618, for instance, the Howard faction dangled William Monson before James. Although they 'took great pains in tricking and pranking him up, beside washing his face every day with posset curd', these nostrums so irritated the king that he immediately dismissed the lad from court. Another attempt six years later ended equally disastrously. When Lionel Cranfield, the Earl of Middlesex, persuaded his brother-in-law, Arthur Brett, to lay his hand upon the king's stirrup whilst they were out hunting, James angrily galloped away.[34]

Buckingham retained the king's favour because he was able to change the nature of their relationship from that of a lover to one in which James saw the favourite as 'my sweet child and wife' while describing himself as 'your old dad and husband'.[35] In Buckingham James first found a lover, and then discovered a mock son, who lacked Prince Henry's priggish independence and Prince Charles's feeble anonymity. Unlike a real heir Buckingham was not impatiently waiting for his father's death and his own inheritance. To the contrary he was fully aware of the problems involved in trying to transfer his hegemony from one reign to another, and never forgot the lesson of the Overbury affair that the king could dismiss a favourite. Buckingham had charm enough to soothe the ageing monarch's irritability (which was in part a product of the piles and porphyria from which James suffered). He even acted as a conduit between the monarch and his estranged family. In return James happily adopted the whole Villiers clan, which he promised 'to advance before all others'. He supported Buckingham's marriage to Lady Katherine Manners, the richest, if not fairest heiress in the land, and let their brats run

through the royal palaces 'like rabbit conies about their burrows' –
antics he never tolerated from his own children.

Because Buckingham's rise in royal favour was so rapid, and was
based on attributes other than political skills, it is not surprising that
in the long term his dominion was disastrous. He monopolized
political power, destroyed his rivals, and thus ended the policy of
having competing factions at court that provided the crown with
alternatives. In the past this policy had permitted Elizabeth I, for
instance, to cut overblown courtiers down to size – as the Earl of
Essex fatally discovered. But now James permitted Buckingham to
entangle England in an adventurous foreign policy that necessitated
calling parliament in a vain attempt to raise taxes to pay for troops.
When Buckingham's military escapades ended in disaster, the crown
returned to the commons to request more money, which precipitated
a constitutional crisis of the first order. The full effects of this ill-
begotten policy, however, were not fully felt until after James's death
in 1625.

It is ironic that the lover of England's most promiscuously homosexual king should have also won the favour of its most uxoriously
prissy sovereign. Initially Charles hated his father's catamite. The
two quarrelled over silly matters. When Charles lost a ring that
Buckingham had lent him, James publicly humiliated the lad. When
Charles turned on a fountain hidden in a statue of Bacchus thus
soaking the favourite as he was out walking with James in the gardens
of Greenwich Palace, the king boxed his son's ears. Gradually Buckingham accepted Sir Francis Bacon's warnings of the political dangers
of being on bad terms with the heir to an ailing monarch, and in
1618 made overtures to which Charles avidly responded. By the end
of that year the prince signed a billet doux to Buckingham as 'your
true constant, loving friend'.[36]

While Buckingham may have appealed to that mildly homosexual
phase that most adolescents experience, Charles also found in him a
substitute for the elder brother, Prince Henry, who had suddenly
died half a dozen years earlier. Buckingham was an entrée to a whole
new exciting adult world. He protected the prince from paternal
anger. He helped him in 1623 when they returned in humiliation
from Madrid after failing personally to woo the King of Spain's
sister. When Charles's marriage to the French princess, Henrietta
Maria, seemed to be floundering, Buckingham was there, ready to
assist his sovereign, just as faithfully as he had when parliament
dared attack the royal prerogative.

'Neither God, nor angel, but a man like any other'

It is not surprising that Charles was distraught when, in 1628, after a long constitutional crisis and three badly botched military expeditions abroad, a crazed army officer, John Felton, assassinated the Duke. Deeply hurt by public rejoicing over the duke's murder, and what he regarded as the intransigence of the House of Commons, the king retired to the world of his court, where he spent much of the 1630s. His marriage with Henrietta Maria improved, they started a family, and through the poems and plays they commissioned they stressed the superiority of platonic love over carnal coupling:

> *When essence meets with essence and souls join*
> *In mutual knots, that's the true nuptial twine*[37]

As the Earl of Castlehaven found out when Charles refused to commute his death sentence for buggery and rape, the new court was a very different place from the old. Indeed the only vice that puritans such as John Milton every attributed to the king was reading too much Shakespeare!

From 1647 to 1648, as a prisoner in Carisbrook Castle in the Isle of Wight, Charles had more than enough time to read the Bard. Parliament had defeated him during the civil war, destroyed the Church of England, driven his wife and two eldest children into exile, and imprisoned his two youngest ones. During this nadir Charles had a deep and most curious affair.

To describe Jane Whorwood as Charles's mistress would be to give their relationship a specificity which can never be fully known. Very little of their correspondence has survived; most of that which remains consists of extremely guarded notes through third parties. Yet their letters give the impression that while neither fully understood what was happening between each other, it both frightened and intrigued them.

Jane was the daughter of William Ryder of Kingston-upon-Thames, a surveyor of James I's stables. In 1634 at the age of nineteen she married Brome, the eldest son of Sir Thomas Whorwood of Holton, Oxfordshire. By the end of the civil war it appears that either their marriage had broken down, that Brome was an ultra-royalist, that he was an exceedingly accommodating husband, or else a remarkably indifferent one.

In late 1647 Alderman Thomas Adams, leader of the City of London's royalists, sent Jane to Hampton Court to give the king half the £1,000 he had collected for the king's use. Apparently she

8 *Charles I and his family*, painted by Hendrick Gerritsz Pot, 1632 (By gracious permission of Her Majesty The Queen)

so impressed Charles that he was happy to use her as a courier for the balance of the money. After she followed the king to the Isle of Wight in the summer of 1648 their relationship blossomed. On 26 July the king wrote to 'Sweet Jane Whorwood' suggesting that she come to meet him in his room supposedly 'by accident'. He signed the letter, 'your most loving Charles'. He was soon calling himself 'her best Platonic lover or Servant'.[38] Over the next few weeks Charles sent Jane at least sixteen messages and met her several more times, outwitting his military guards. In August he begged her not to leave the Isle of Wight. 'Tell Jane Whorwood', he asked a mutual friend that 'her Platonic Way doth much spoil the taste of my mind.' By the following month Jane seemed to have mended her ways (platonic or otherwise), for she called Charles 'my dear friend', and signed herself with the *nom d'amour* 'Your most affectionate Helen'.[39]

Charles was a lonely, dependent prisoner. Jane was a loving woman and a loyal subject, capable of arousing the king's limited capacity for friendship and affection. Although he assured Jane that he would tell his wife all about her, Charles never did so – always a sign of a guilty conscience, if not worse. So if we cannot say for sure what role she played physically, there is no doubt that emotionally Jane had a profound effect on the martyr king. As he bade her farewell in his last letter he said 'she had given him great contentment'.[40]

As Charles steeled himself for the ordeal of his trial and execution he needed all the contentment he could garner. Yet had he as a free king shown but a fraction of the capacity for love and friendship he displayed toward Mistress Whorwood as a close prisoner, Charles I might never have ended his life on the scaffold. And that was a lesson his son, Charles II, never forgot.

V

'NEVER LAY HANDS UPON HIS SCEPTRE'

No sovereign has sailed a happier voyage than the one which Charles II took from Schevenigen, Holland, to Dover in May of 1660. Aboard ship the new monarch talked gaily about his adventures in exile, and his dealings with the hectoring Scots Presbyterians. He recalled his defeat at Worcester in 1650 and ensuing escape, and his escapades afterwards as a refugee on the continent when at times he seemed to be trying to drown the paucity of his hopes with draughts of libidinal pleasures. At the conclusion of this happy return he landed at Dover, to be welcomed by General Monck, the soldier who ended the ailing Cromwellian republic and restored the monarchy. The Mayor of Dover presented the returned sovereign with a copy of the Authorized Version of the Bible which Charles, with the good manners which were the hallmark of his personality, declared was 'the thing he loved above all other things in the world'.[1]

After a triumphant journey through Kent, the king entered London on 29 May, his thirtieth birthday. According to one eyewitness the people's joy was 'inexpressible'. When an inn-keeper's wife became so excited that she gave birth, Charles graciously stopped the procession to welcome his newest subject. The Lord Mayor and Alderman, wearing their gold chains of office and purple liveries waited at the city gates to receive the king. The streets were strewn with flowers and filled with the happy sounds of music and people rejoicing that it 'was the Lord's doing'. John Evelyn, the diarist, thought that there had never been such a restoration 'since the return of the Jews from the Babylonian captivity'.[2]

9 *Charles II*, father of fourteen acknowledged bastards but no legitimate heirs. Attributed to Thomas Hawker, 1680 (National Portrait Gallery)

All England but one Bonfire seems to be,
One Aetna shooting flames into the sea.

And that evening the new monarch celebrated the first night in his capital with his mistress, Barbara Palmer, by siring their first child, Anne.

Posterity has viewed the restoration of the monarchy with nearly as much enthusiasm as its contemporaries. It marked the end of a long night of Puritan repression and military misrule. No longer would Englishmen be denied their rights to celebrate Christmas and dance around Maypoles. No more would they groan under the tyranny of jumped-up apprentice boys promoted major generals. Merrie England was theirs again, and would be kept safe so long as the army knew its place, never again meddling in politics, and so long as God saved the king and confounded the knavish tricks of republicans.

The Restoration centred around one king, Charles II. Far from making him bitter, his exile and his father's execution had rather made him more careful. If he sought solace in the arms of many women during this ordeal, he at least kept his sense of humour, his courtesy, and his ability to ensure that he would never again embark on his travels. Before 1660 the women he enjoyed, and the bastards he sired, taught him the patience which did much to bring about his return. After 1660 his mistresses were not merely relaxations from the tensions of trying to remain in power but permitted him to pursue alternative policies, while keeping his options open.

For a man who had so many illegitimate affairs and children, Charles set a surprisingly high premium on legitimacy. Because he had no issue by his wife, Catherine of Braganza, he insisted that his brother, the Catholic James II, inherit the throne. A greater contrast between two siblings could not have been found, for while James was equally as promiscuous, he was tormented with such an intense sense of guilt that it may well have paralysed him and resulted in his deposition in 1688.

Half a century earlier civil wars, a restoration, and a revolution (glorious or not) were the last things on people's minds when Charles I and Henrietta Maria had their first child in May 1630. While trying to conceal his joy, the new father ordered several of his opponents freed from prison, gave London £100 for the relief of plague victims, and had the baby christened with great pomp a month later. Most agreed that the very bright appearance of Venus at the time of the baby's birth was an auspicious (and as it turned out) appropriate omen. But the babe's mother was not so sure. 'He is so fat and so tall', Henrietta Maria wrote to a friend 'and so dark that I am ashamed of him.'[3]

The king and queen were not particularly good parents, especially to their first two children, Charles and James. Until the last few months of his life, Charles lacked the informality needed to be a good father. When his children were young he had their portrait by Van Dyck hung above his breakfast table where they could be seen but not heard.

Charles II's governor had more influence on his childhood development than his father. The Earl of Newcastle was a cultivated grandee who did not over-burden the boy with too much learning. Instead he taught him that it was vital for a monarch 'to be most courteous and civil to everybody', and that 'to women you cannot be too civil, especially to great ones'.[4]

The civil war further separated the king from his heir. Prince Charles and Prince James spent the first two years of the conflict with their father in the royalist headquarters of Oxford. The king let them watch the Battle of Edgehill with William Harvey, the great physician, (who became too engrossed in a book to notice the cannon balls that fell close to his precious charges). In 1644, as his fortunes hung in the balance, Charles I sent his eleven-year-old heir to the West Country to serve as titular head of the royalist forces. Two years later, the defeat at Naseby having sealed the royalist fate, Prince Charles sailed from Cornwall, first to the Scilly Islands, and then Jersey. Four months afterwards, having rejected his counsellors' advice that leaving this last royalist stronghold would greatly diminish the morale of the last-ditch cavaliers still fighting in England, the prince sailed for France. In 1648, sick and tired of his mother's interference (she pocketed his pension from Cardinal Mazarin saying that no English heir should stoop so low as to accept a French dole), Charles left her to go to Holland.

The young prince had not been away from his father's supervision for long before he made the acquaintance of what he later referred to as that 'little fantastical gentleman called cupid'.[5] Charles was only fifteen when Christabella Wyndham, the wife of the royalist governor of Bridgewater, seduced him. Since Christabella had been one of his wet nurses as a baby, this initiation might well interest modern Freudians: certainly it outraged the princes's chief adviser, Edward Hyde, who was shocked when Mrs Wyndham, 'a woman of great rudeness and country pride', maternally kissed the prince in public.[6]

Charles's next love, Marguerite Carteret, was but four years his senior. The daughter of the Seigneur of Trinity Manor, she first met the prince in Jersey in early 1646. Afterwards she claimed that her son James was the product of this encounter, which seems unlikely, for Charles usually acknowledged his bastards. Anyway the pregnant Marguerite hurried to marry Jean de la Cloche, an obscure fellow, well enough below her station to be happy to agree to be the father of someone else's child.

Charles proudly recognized the off-spring of his next liaison, with Lucy Walters. Evelyn described her as 'a brown, beautiful, bold, but insipid creature', while Hyde thought Lucy was a 'welsh woman of no good fame but handsome'.[7] She first met Charles in the Hague in 1648 and became pregnant by him in July. Subsequently she claimed to have married Charles, thus attempting to legitimize their son James a few months before his birth the following April – an assertion that Charles denied, and which Lucy's later behaviour belied. After staying with Charles, mainly in Paris, for a couple of years, she left him for a legion of lovers, any one of whom could have fathered her next two children. When her eldest child, James, was seven Lucy returned to England. The Cromwellian regime arrested her, and after taking full advantage of this propaganda coup to discredit the pretender's morals, deported her to the continent, where, after Charles seized custody of their son, she died of venereal disease in 1658.

During his exile Charles's relations with his other mistresses were as amiable as those with Lucy were acrimonious. In 1651 he had a daughter, Charlotte Fitzroy, by Elizabeth Killigrew, who was the sister of the Duke of York's chaplain, and the wife of Francis Boyle, Viscount Shannon. Seven years later he and Catherine Pegge, the daughter of a Derbyshire squire, had a daughter, who died in infancy, and a son, Charles Fitzroy, who survived. At the same time Charles conducted a discrete liaison with the twice-widowed Lady Elizabeth Byron.

Such promiscuity scandalized the Puritans. One Cromwellian spy lumped 'fornication, drunkenness and adultery' together with going to the theatre on the sabbath, as the 'great abominations' that 'are esteemed no sin' amongst the prince and his cronies.[8] But for Charles the activities relieved both the tensions of war, and the despair of defeat. If mistresses – and one of them claimed she was his seventeenth – did not keep the exiled heir going during the dark days of the Commonwealth, they did at least help him retain that sense of humour and those cheerful good manners that did so much to endear him to his fellow countrymen when the monarchy was restored in 1660.

When he returned to claim his patrimony the new king did not, of course, leave his promiscuous ways behind on the continent; instead he brought with him his current mistress, Barbara Palmer. She was born in 1640, a member of the Villiers family, her grandfather, Grandison, being half-brother to the Duke of Buckingham, James I's favourite. Her father, also christened Grandison, was a typical cavalier: brave, handsome, married to a beautiful heiress, he went to the wars with all the enthusiasm of a golden innocent. Immediately after his sovereign raised the royal standard at Nottingham, Grandison recruited a regiment of cavalry, and started to harry the rebels. Taken prisoner at Winchester, he escaped to see action at Edgehill, where his regiment recaptured the royal standard taken from the slain Sir Edmund Verney. Whilst fighting with equal valour at the siege of Bristol, he was wounded in the thigh. A few weeks later he died at Oxford and was buried in Christ Church.

Perhaps it was her father's sense of adventure, or else his loss when she was two years old, that helped turn Barbara into what the Count de Grammont (with uncharacteristically Gallic understatement) described as 'a lively and demanding woman'.[9] She lost her virginity to Philip Stanhope, the second Earl of Chesterfield, a violent fellow who had murdered a man in a duel over the return of a horse. After he left her to marry the Duke of Ormond's daughter for a large dowry, Barbara was furious, cutting him dead. 'After so many years service, fidelity and respect',[10] the earl protested, 'to be banished for the first offence is very hard.'

But by no stretch of the imagination could Barbara be described as a first offender: indeed so accomplished was this young houri that one courtier, alluding to the banned sonnets of Pietro Aretino which with poetry and pictures illustrated sixteen sexual positions, declared that she knew 'all the tricks of Aretin'.[11]

In 1659 Barbara seemed to forsake her torrid past by marrying Roger Palmer, an ardently royalist law student. The couple came to Holland to serve their sovereign over the waters and stayed with him when he returned to England. Roger's bride was, perhaps, of greater service. She captivated the king with her engaging laugh, and exactly nine months after the restoration, on 25 February 1661, gave

10 *Barbara Palmer, Lady Castlemaine*, 'a lively and demanding woman'. Miniature by Samuel Cooper (By gracious permission of Her Majesty The Queen)

birth to a daughter, Anne, whom Charles immediately acknowledged as his own. Ten months afterwards, at Barbara's insistence, Charles awarded her husband an earl's coronet to crown his cuckold's horns. But the patent creating Roger Lord Castlemaine vested the peerage to the heirs of her ladyship's body – 'the reason whereof everyone knows', was Samuel Pepys's snide comment.[12]

Charles soon came to realize the universally recognized truth that as a single man possessing the good fortune of having been restored to the throne, he was in want of a wife to produce an heir. But, unlike Jane Austen, Charles was neither too proud nor prejudiced to think that taking a wife meant extinguishing his old flames. Thus inclined he started enquiring about prospective brides. The Prince of Parma's eldest daughter was reported as very ugly, while the youngest was 'monstrous big'. While Charles personally rejected a bevy of German princesses, because 'they are all dull and foggy',[13] there is no evidence that he accepted Catherine of Braganza because she was either bright or clear.

The allures of the King of Portugal's daughter were financial rather than physical: a huge dowry worth some £360,000, as well as the ports of Tangier and Bombay, and lucrative trading privileges in the new world. On seeing his wife for the first time, her hair dressed in the Portuguese fashion, with corkscrew braids coming out on either side of her head, Charles was horrified. 'I thought that they had brought me a bat instead of a woman', he confided to a friend.[14] A little later a court wit described the queen:

> Ill natured little goblin, and designed
> For nothing but to dance and vex mankind.

After their wedding in Portsmouth on 23 May 1662, and a disappointing wedding night, Charles treated his wife so kindly that several speculated that the marriage might actually work, 'Which I fear', noted Pepys, 'will put Madam Castlemaine's nose out of joint.'[15]

Putting Lady Castlemaine out of her husband's bed had always been one of Catherine's goals. Her first reaction on learning she was to be married to the King of England, a heretic, was to go on a pilgrimage to a saint's shrine; her second was to promise her mother she would not tolerate her espoused's paramours.

Unfortunately Charles had made an equally solemn promise to Barbara to make her one of the new queen's ladies-in-waiting. Since she had just presented him with a son, and – unlike Catherine – did not surround herself with a dismal train of numerous confessors, a deaf duenna, a Jewish perfumer, and a gaggle of 'old, ugly and proud' servants (all badly in need of a wash), the king was much more inclined to keep his promise to his mistress than to his wife.

Barbara was not, however, content to pin her hopes solely upon her sovereign's inclinations, but treated the new queen with public disdain. For instance, she refused to light a bonfire to celebrate the royal wedding, and quite literally washed her dirty linen in public, by hanging her frilly undergarments out on the line to dry – much to Pepys's titillation, the lingerie being the finest 'I ever saw, and did me much good to look at them'.[16]

Barbara also insisted on being presented to the queen at court. At first Catherine, whose English was still rusty, did not recognize her, but when she realized that she had just been introduced to her rival, she turned white, sobbed, her nose started to bleed, and she fainted. Charles was adamant. He cut his wife. He sent her servants back to Portugal. He brushed aside her threats to go home to mother. At court the queen was ignored, or worst still became the target for sniggers – 'the king kept her for breeding'[17] was the Earl of Rochester's catty conclusion. Charles made it quite clear that 'whosoever I find to be my Lady Castlemaine's enemy in this matter, I do promise upon my word to be his enemy so long as I live'.[18] After Edward Hyde, recently promoted Earl of Clarendon, failed to reconcile the couple, Catherine suddenly capitulated by publicly receiving her rival.

Because he sought his pleasures elsewhere, Charles had little expectation from marriage. As he told his brother, a wife's beauty 'contributes nothing to, and takes nothing from, the happiness of marriage, and in a week one gets so accustomed to her face that it neither pleases nor displeases one'. From such minuscule expectations the royal marriage improved. Fundamentally a kind man, Charles humoured his wife's hallucinations when, desperately ill in 1663, she thought that she had actually given birth to a child. But the fact remained that the queen amounted to little more than Old Rowley's brood-mare who failed to breed.

Such was a marked contrast with Barbara Palmer, who bore Charles a total of five children. Her fecundity – combined with the discarded queen's barrenness – made her even more greedy and promiscuous. Apart from the king, she slept with the Earl of St Albans, and a Miss Hobart (a Maid of Honour, who was also intimate with Charles). She persuaded the king to appoint Dr Henry Glenham, her mother's uncle and a notorious drunkard, Bishop of St Asaph, and to make her old lover, Thomas Wood, Bishop of Coventry. But Barbara went too far – even for a man as tolerant of human foibles as Charles II – when she made love to both Jacob Hall, a rope dancer, in his booth at St Bartholomew's Fair, and with an anonymous footman in her bath. The last straw came when she then insisted that the king acknowledge the paternity of her children, no matter how and with whom they had been conceived.

Perhaps it was Barbara's growing promiscuity that helped attract Charles to Frances Stewart, a strikingly innocent maid, who came to court after a French education to serve as one of Queen Catherine's maids of honour. Without doubt she was a beautiful woman, with a fine figure, and slim legs which she showed off to great effect by wearing men's clothes. Princess Henriette-Anne called her 'the prettiest girl imaginable', while Pepys thought her 'a glorious sight'.[19] Charles agreed, using her as the model for Britannia, whose effigy adorned England's pennies for centuries.

But Frances's most unique characteristic was neither her beauty – for there were many exquisite women at Charles's court, nor was it her wit and gaiety – since those were qualities that the royal palaces had in legion. Rather it was that most uncommon virtue – chastity. Frances was one of the very few women at court whom Lely could use as a model to paint the mythical Diana without prompting cynical titters.

It was this rare commodity that attracted Charles and worried Barbara. As with Henry VIII, maidenly refusal added petrol to the royal fires. Passionately, Charles sighed:

> O then, 'tis then, that I think there's no hell
> Like loving, like loving too well.[20]

To forestall her rival Barbara played a dangerous game. She and Frances took part in a 'mock marriage' complete with a ceremonial bedding. This gave the king an excuse to view the younger woman sleeping, and the older the opportunity to play the role of the senior mistress, who controlled her lover through the junior.

Such a scheme was not so far fetched. When Madame de Pompadour found that age and childbearing eroded her physical allures and thus threatened her hegemony as *maîtresse en titre* to Louis XIV, she recruited a stable of younger woman. She housed them at Versailles and told them that their visitor was a Polish nobleman who for the highest reasons of state must remain incognito. Only one girl discovered the truth, and she was consigned to a lunatic asylum.

But Charles was neither so gullible, nor was Frances so co-operative. After resisting the king's advances for a couple of years, she escaped from the torrid hothouse of the court by eloping with the Duke of Richmond. The king was deeply hurt, particularly as the duke was widely regarded as a pretty dull fellow. He told his sister, 'I cannot so soon forget the injury which went so near my heart', and banished the couple from his presence. But when Frances caught smallpox the following year Charles's basic good nature reasserted itself. When she recovered, her beauty having been spared the usual blight of facial pox-marks, the king received Frances and her husband back at court.

Charles had been badly frightened. Having loved Frances so well – but not at all, and Barbara so often – and yet so badly, he was determined to permit no woman to monopolize either his affections or his bed. In much the same fashion, by dismissing Clarendon in 1667, he was sending just as clear a signal that no minister would again dominate his counsels.

Over the next few years the king had a number of affairs, none of which amounted to much. There was Winifred Wells, one of the queen's maids of honour, whom one courtier described as 'a big splendidly handsome creature', spoiled only by 'a certain air of indecision which gave her the physiognomy of a dreamy sheep'.[21] (Barbara thought her a goose.) There was Jane Roberts, a clergyman's daughter, who died young, riddled with guilt about her adulteries. Then Charles had Moll Davis, an actress with the morals expected then from her profession – Pepys thought her 'the most impertinent slut'.[22] Moll did not suffer from Jane's guilt. After entertaining the king with her guitar and heavy-faced looks and sensuous lips, she was happy to be discharged with a pension and return to the stage. The king enjoyed the charms of Mary Killegrew, the widowed Countess of Falmouth, before she went on to marry Lord Buckhurst, as well as those of Elizabeth, Countess of Kildare. And there were the troops of nameless ladies. William Chaffinch, the Keeper of the Closet, would arrange for them to land at night at the palace steps beneath the king's bedchamber overlooking the Thames, or else walk over the road from the inappropriately named Maiden's Inn to the country house that Charles built for himself at Newmarket.

It was inevitable that the consensus which attended the restoration of the monarchy in 1660 should eventually break down, and the strains that helped produce the civil war during the 1640s should reappear. After Charles permitted the Church of England to dominate England's religious and political life – much as his father had allowed Archbishop Laud in the 1630s – a new divisiveness emerged that pitted Tory against Whig, and Catholics, Anglicans and Nonconformists against each other. For many, the shibboleth of loyalty was foreign policy. Whigs tended to support an alliance with Protestant Holland, while Tories favoured one with Catholic France.

The king's extra-marital affairs reflected these divisions.

Charles first met Louise de Kéroüalle in 1670, when the beautiful young Breton girl came over to England with his sister, Henriette-Anne. Fourteen years his junior, Henriette-Anne had always been his favourite. He nicknamed her 'Minette', writing her long letters in which he revealed his innermost secrets, including those of his wedding night. Poor Minette was unhappily married to the Duke of Orleans, a homosexual homicidal maniac who liked strutting around wearing high-heeled shoes, perfume, and rouge. Thus when Minette was able to escape her French husband to return home on a diplomatic mission, Charles was overjoyed to see her. He was also enamoured with her lady-in-waiting, and tried to persuade Minette to leave Louise behind in England. But his sister refused, saying that she had promised the girl's parents to return Louise home safely.

After a tearful farewell at Dover, in which Charles thrice reboarded the vessel taking Henriette-Anne back to France for one last embrace, brother and sister parted. Three weeks later Henriette-Anne died of peritonitis. Charles was devastated. He had lost the love of his life, the woman whom he admired above all others. She was the one with whom he could feel completely at ease, with whom he could be utterly honest if only because as a sister he could enjoy her without the impermanent allure and inevitable guilt of a sexual relationship. He could neither seduce Minette, nor had he every night to prove himself to her. Neither need he worry about her growing old, or being displaced by younger rivals, for theirs was a relationship of birth which only death could end.

Recognizing the depth of Charles's despair, as well as the intensity of his infatuation, Louis XIV sent Louise de Kéroüalle back to England. At first she clung to her virginity, asking about Catherine of Braganza's health – perhaps in the hope that the King of England might soon become a widower able to marry her. The best she could obtain was 'a mock marriage' at Euston Hall in October 1671, during which she and Charles threw a stocking to the courtiers waiting outside their bedroom to symbolize the consummation of their union. Of that there was little doubt. The following month Louis XIV congratulated her for a mission well done. Nine months later Louise gave birth to a son, Charles, whom the king delightedly acknowledged as his own. He made the boy's mother Duchess of Portsmouth, gave her a pension of £10,000 a year and a suite of twenty-four rooms in Whitehall Palace.

> *Within this place a bed's appointed*
> *For a French bitch and God's anointed.*[23]

So ran an anonymous libel pinned on their apartment door.

While by no reckoning could the new mistress be described as beautiful, or even voluptuous, she possessed a most erotic innocence. Evelyn thought she had 'a childish, simple and baby face'.[24] Henri Gascar's portrait shows a pretty woman with thick inviting lips, proud looks, and masses of dark, rolling curls. Coyly, a small breast is revealed, while underneath, perhaps as a symbol of her diplomatic mission, she holds a dove. The portrait does not reveal any eye impediment, belying Nell Gwynn's bitchy epitaph 'squintabella'. But her chubby cheeks and neck explain why Charles nicknamed her 'Fubbs'.

While Louise's innocent sexuality first attracted the king, it was her ability to provide him with a sense of domestic permanence which kept her Charles's mistress for the rest of his life. She provided him with a welcoming set of rooms, an exciting bed, a sympathetic ear, and one of the best tables in the land. Instinctively she realized that her lover – who had just turned forty – wanted a sense of comfortable stability, that snug harbour which men seek when they realize their lives will not go on for ever. Yet she also recognized that Charles did not want to feel too comfortable. She sensed that he could neither escape, nor wanted to be completely free from the undertow of lingering guilt that was an inevitable part of all his affairs. Thus, to control her lover, Louise threw public tantrums and put on so many fits of tearful hysteria that Nell Gwynn astutely called her 'the weeping willow'.

Most observers were convinced that Louise utterly dominated the king. Sir John Reresby, a connoisseur of other men's wives, called her 'the most absolute of the king's mistresses'. For a bribe she had Ralph Brideoake made Bishop of Chichester, and allegedly helped

11 *Louise de Kéroüalle, Duchess of Portsmouth,* 'the most absolute of the king's mistresses' by Vignon (By gracious permission of Her Majesty The Queen)

start the legal career of George Jeffreys (who eventually became the notorious judge of the bloody assizes). 'No body shall come to Court or to any preferment', boasted Louise, 'but those who will be my creatures.'[25]

Many Englishmen accepted her extravagant claims. After all, during her hegemony Charles adopted a pro-French foreign policy, even signing the secret Treaty of Dover by which the King of England became Louis XIV's pensioner. Thus the arrival of Hortense Mancini in England in late 1675 encouraged those who opposed the pro-French drift of the king's policies.

In her late twenties Hortense was one of the most beautiful women in Europe, with an air of flamboyant mystique that many found irresistible. She was the niece of Cardinal Mazarin, who had elevated her first husband to Duke of Mazarin. But the duke was a religious maniac, who forced her to perform the most extravagant penances for all their sins – real or imagined, so she left him. But when Louis XIV refused to respond to her petitions that her husband return the property she had brought to their marriage, Hortense became one of the French monarch's most implacable enemies. After a brief dalliance with the Duke of Savoy, she turned up in England, complete with her black page, Mustapha, and a pet parrot. This aristocratic Italian beauty, with a classic profile and dark hair, could have reminded Charles of Barbara Palmer. Or else their affair might have been an attempt to recapture a youthful passion, for the king promptly installed Hortense in Barbara's old apartments.

This new infatuation worried Louise de Kéroüalle as sorely as it did her allies. The French ambassador wrote home that Paris was about to lose all its influence in London. Such a demise delighted Nell Gwynn, who as the Protestant totem triumphantly staged a mock funeral.

Neither the dictates of *realpolitiks*, nor the pranks of orange-sellers, ended Hortense's brief but glorious career as the King of England's mistress. Instead her own instability brought it crashing down. Hortense was a compulsive gambler, an ardent athlete, a fine shot, and a nymphomaniac. 'Each sex provides its lovers for Hortense', a courtier observed. She became over-familiar with Charles's daughter, Anne, by Barbara Palmer, to the understandable annoyance of her father and husband. In the summer of 1677 Hortense finally alienated the king by outrageously flirting with the Prince of Monaco.

Having dismissed the flamboyant Frenchwoman, Charles's

relations returned to their normal pattern. He enjoyed Louise de Kéroüalle's domestic stability, almost as if she were the stable loving wife whom he never found in the queen, while turning to Nell Gwynn for that sparkle which middle-aged men often seek from a courtesan.

Nell Gwynn was the best known of the king's mistresses. Small bodied, with the long slender legs which Charles always liked, generous breasts, a heart-shaped face, hazel eyes, and chestnut brown hair, Nell was an extremely attractive woman. She was of Welsh extraction. Her father had died in an Oxford prison; her mother had kept a high class brothel where young Nell first served drinks, and then herself. Soon she graduated to becoming an orange-seller at the King's Theatre, a profession which bordered on the oldest. Illiterate, she used the only talents her Maker had given her – a fine body and a sharp wit.

Before meeting the king, she had numerous lovers, supposedly seducing the poet John Dryden. A successful actress, she was the rage of the London stage: Pepys was infatuated after seeing her as Florimel in Dryden's *Maiden Queen*. Others, higher born than the diligent diarist, were more fully able to enjoy her charms. Nell became mistress first to Charles Hart, and second to Charles, Lord Buckhurst – which prompted her to teasingly call the king 'My Charles the Third'.[26]

Like most of her lovers, Charles did not appear to mind, for Nell had a cheerfully open honesty that allowed her to stay friends with her men long after their dalliances were done. On bearing a son, Charles, Duke of St Albans, in 1670, her place in the king's affections was secure. She remained faithful to him for the rest of her life. Charles repaid the compliment, for as he lay dying in 1685 he begged his brother James to 'not let poor Nelly starve'.

The king died leaving no legitimate children, but some fourteen acknowledged bastards, by seven mothers. So numerous had been his affairs, that when someone asked him how many women he had, Charles mischievously answered thirty-nine, explaining that the number of articles of the Anglican Faith was a good enough total for the head of the Church of England.

But like those articles, Charles's mistresses had little direct influence. Some thought otherwise. John Wilmot, the Earl of Rochester, the wit whose malice always exceeded his reliability, wrote:

12 *Nell Gwynn*, the popular 'Protestant whore'. Engraving after Simon Verelst (Mary Evans Picture Library)

Nor are his high Desires above his strength,
His Sceptre and his prick are a length,
And she may sway the one who plays with the other,
And makes him little wiser than his brother.[27]

The French ambassador Colbert de Croissy, assumed that Charles's paramours had the same influence as his own sovereign's *maîtresses en titre*, and thus tried to buy their influence. He was wasting his money, for the doggerel verse about Nell Gwynn basically applied to them all:

She hath got a trick to handle his prick
But never lay hands upon his sceptre.[28]

On the other hand, the indirect political effects of Charles's amorous activities were far from inconsiderable.

Charles was, quite simply, a man who loved women, and a man whom women loved. Of course, as a king he had the allure that attends all men with power, and the money to gratify his tastes. But personally he was a very attractive man. In spite of his protestation 'Odd's fish, I am an ugly fellow', women found him irresistible, and (if Barbara Palmer is to be believed) well endowed. Certainly he relished his nickname of 'Old Rowley', taken from one of the stallions in the royal stud.

But the king not only liked women; he liked all his fellow creatures, behaving towards them with that easy familiarity that his ill-fated father so conspicuously lacked. As Andrew Marvell noted, Charles II treated his mistresses and their offspring with marked generosity:

The misses take place, each advanced to be a duchess.
With pomp as great as queens in their coach and six horses,
The bastards made dukes, earls, viscounts and lords,
With all the title that honour affords.[29]

And when the affair was over Charles usually parted on good terms with those he had loved, for he had that uniquely valuable quality in a ruler of being able to discard people, – be they lovers, petitioners, or ministers – with the minimum of fuss and ill-feeling. Unlike his father he had no stubborn commitment to either policies or people, being able to embrace and discard both with a grace that offended few.

There was something endearingly human about all the king's activities. He did not have the stultifying formality of his father's court, nor the extravagant rituals of Louis XIV's Versailles. Indeed he scorned such pretensions, once remarking that the King of Spain was so stuck-up that he 'would not piss but another must hold the chamber pot'.[30] Being teased by Nell Gwynn that England's second Charles was her third, or having to deal with Barbara's tantrums, or his own illegitimate children's problems, reminded the king of the ordinary difficulties his subjects faced in their daily round. It helped curb the absolutist tendencies of his time. Having several mistresses let people associate a specific royal policy with a particular woman. In a sense she became the totem for various factions. Just as Charles's many liaisons had been an escape during the dark days of exile, so at the end of his reign his 'family' of Nell Gwynn and Louise de Kéroüalle became comfortable havens from the storms of the Papist Plot and the Exclusion Crisis outside.

While the king's many – and well known – affairs were bound to influence public opinion, how precisely they did so is hard to say. Some people were, of course, horrified: but there was no way that any monarch, no matter how saintly, could have pleased the likes of a Milton or Bunyan.

Men of less puritanical mettle protested against the king's affairs more on the grounds of expense than morality. Andrew Marvell complained about the extravagant establishment the king gave Hortense Mancini, after he had already provided Louise de Kéroüalle with an equally expensive love-nest.

> *That the king should send for another French whore*
> *When one already had made him so poor.*[31]

Many felt Barbara Palmer had gone too far when she expected the king and ultimately the exchequer to support all her bastards regardless of their paternity. Some compared her to Jane Shore, Edward IV's mistress, who had been punished for her promiscuity.[32]

> *The reason why she is not duck'd*
> *Because by Caesar she is fucked.*

Thus ran a libel posted on Barbara's door, the author of which not even £1,000 reward could discover. In 1667 several thousand London apprentices – a group not noted for excessive sexual prudery – rioted for days in part to protest at Barbara's pretensions. After destroying several of the city's brothels, they started chanting 'why do we not pull down the great one at Whitehall?' As always the rioters demands became confused, and the fracas degenerated into a general attack on royal policy, toieration of non-conformity being a particular grievance.

Samuel Pepys, who recorded the young men's protests in his diary and thought the complaints of *The Poor Whores' Petition* about unfair competition from court were 'not very witty, but devilish sincere', expressed the ambivalence that many of Charles's subjects felt towards the monarch's affairs. 'There is nothing almost but bawdy at Court from top to bottom', fulminated one observer, while another described it as 'The Court of Cuckolds'. Pepys complained about 'the lewdness and beggary of this court, which I am feared will bring all to ruin again'. Yet more often he relished the king's pretty paramours, particularly Nell Gwynn and Barbara Palmer. Once he had a dream, 'the best that was ever dreamed', of having 'My Lady Castlemaine in my arms, and was admitted to use all the dalliance I desired with her'.[33]

Pepys was not alone in his fantasies of sleeping with his monarch's whores, for loyal (and presumably slightly envious) subjects bought paintings of them, which, like modern pin-ups, hid few attractions. Thus as a whole it seems safe to assume that the diarist's approval of his monarch's trysts was typical, if only because it was in keeping with the spirit of the times.

The Restoration was a liberation from the restrictions of the Commonwealth, which as the years passed seemed to grow more onerous. A dozen years after the Puritans had in 1650 passed 'An act for Suppressing the Detestable Sins of Incest, Adultery and Fornication' that prescribed for offenders 'death as in case of Felony', cavalier poets and playwrights pandered to the age's new morality – or lack thereof – replacing that ugly word 'adultery' with the euphemistic 'gallantry'.[34] So common had the keeping of mistresses become that a character in Dryden's play *Marriage à la Mode* complained that because demand so exceeded supply 'poor little creatures without beauty, birth or breeding, but only impudence, go off at unreasonable rates'.[35] Pepys's brother 'told us a thing certain that the Archbishop of Canterbury that now is doth keep a wench'.[36] The court symbolized this new permissive society. So vital a status symbol had maintaining a mistress become that a wag warned Francis North, the middle-aged Lord Keeper, that if he did not acquire one he 'would lose all his interest at court'.

Like the other highly procreative English monarch, Henry I, the supreme irony of Charles II's reign was that he had no legitimate male heir, and died leaving a serious succession problem. Had Charles enjoyed a better reputation as a young man in exile, Amelia of Solms might have allowed his engagement to her daughter Princess Henrietta Catherine of Orange to stand, and he would have married a woman who turned out to be far more fertile than his wife, Catherine of Braganza. Even though Charles did not suffer from that intense sense of guilt that plagued his father, he did not escape as unscathed as his flippancy to Bishop Burnet that 'surely God would never damn a man for allowing himself a little pleasure', would suggest. The king's feelings towards his wife were those of guilt, mitigated by pity. 'Alas! Poor woman', he said when someone told him as he lay dying that Catherine of Braganza had asked his forgiveness. 'She beg my pardon! I beg hers with all my heart.'[37]

Paradoxically as the number of his illegitimate offspring increased, Charles's commitment to legitimacy rose. He insisted that his brother, James, fulfil his promise to marry Anne Hyde, the Earl of Clarendon's daughter, after making her pregnant. After James declared he was a Catholic, Charles did all he could to stop parliament from depriving his brother of his lawful inheritance.

James II had just as hearty an appetite for women as had Charles II, although a very much less healthy one. While the elder brother has gone down in history as the merry monarch, the more appropriate epithet for the younger was the one that Nell Gwynn bestowed upon him, 'Dismal Jimmy'. Since neither brother was completely amoral, and both were Christians, their infidelities made them feel guilty. But they expressed their guilt in different fashions. Perhaps Charles's conscience was the more pliable. Certainly it was flexible enough to allow him to remain a secret papist right up until his death bed, when at the last minute he declared his Catholic faith. On the other hand James, who made no secret of his beliefs, seemed to have felt so much guilt that at times he appeared to be neurotically self-destructive, particularly during the greatest crisis of his reign, the Glorious Revolution of 1688.

In many ways the civil war of the 1640s shaped James II. He had never been close to his father. When hostilities started, breaking up the royal family, James became increasingly critical of Charles I's mealy-mouthed stand. Taken prisoner by the parliament, James managed to escape dressed as a girl (something Charles I conspicuously failed to do) from Carisbrook Castle. After his father's execution he remarked that Charles had been his own worse enemy 'by too great a display of leniency'.[38] Such single- (and simple-) mindedness helped James become a distinguished soldier of fortune who fought with great courage in Louis XIV's service, rising to the rank of Leiutenant General.

He was a handsome young man, 'extremely good-looking and well-made and with a fair complexion'. Like his elder brother, James sought relief from the despair of exile in the arms of other women, eventually marrying Anne, the Earl of Clarendon's daughter. One satirist voiced the widely held opinion that the bride's ambitious father had tricked him into this unsuitable union:

> Then the Fat Scrivener doth begin to think
> Twas time to mix the Royal blood with ink.[39]

In fact James married Anne out of a sense of obligation, and because his brother insisted that he keep the promise he made before bedding her. After losing their first child, the cause of their coerced union, they had two daughters, Mary and Anne, (as well as six other children who did not survive). According to Pepys, Anne Hyde was 'a plain woman and like her mother'.[40] Although James was fond of his wife, an intelligent person who did much to bring out his Catholic tendencies, he continued to have affairs, without any respect for Anne's sensitivities. 'He hath come out of his wife's bed, and gone to others laid in bed for him', observed Pepys.[41] And since Anne was a commoner's daughter, she had reluctantly to put up with her husband's infidelities, and, starved of the pleasures of the bed, turned in compensation to those of the table, becoming inordinately fat. She died in 1671.

So hearty were James's sexual appetites that to protect their wives the Earl of Chesterfield and Lord Roberts removed them from court, while the Earl of Southesk had to spread the story that his bride had venereal disease.

James first had a brief fling with Godotha Price, daughter of Sir Herbert Price, Master of the King's Household, and maid of honour to his wife (who was most mortified). Then he took Lady Elizabeth Denham, the wife of the royalist poet, Sir John Denham.

13 *James, Duke of York, later James II, with his first wife Anne Hyde.* Pepys observed 'The Duke of York in all things but his codpiece is led by his wife'. By Sir Peter Lely after 1660 (National Portrait Gallery)

14 *James II*, by Sir Godfrey Kneller 1684–5 (National Portrait Gallery)

During the civil war Sir John Denham had fought bravely for the crown, was taken prisoner, served as a conduit between the imprisoned king and Henrietta Maria, had his lands confiscated, and was driven into exile. At the restoration Charles II rewarded his fidelity with grants of land and revenue, and by appointing him Surveyor General of Works, even though the poet knew nothing about building and architecture. With his fortunes mended, although his health was far from repaired, in 1665 at the age of fifty the poet took a second wife, Margaret, Sir William Brook's eighteen-year-old daughter. Not surprisingly she quickly tired of him, and became James's mistress, much to her husband's distress, particularly as they conducted their trysts openly in his house at Scotland Yard. Such a brazen betrayal unhinged the poor fellow, who complained to the king. The fact that Sir John did so under the impression that he was the Holy Ghost did nothing to enhance the cuckold's case. Neither too, did his young wife's premature death a little later. Many agreed with Pepys that Denham had poisoned her, and the only way he could stop his neighbours in Westminster from tearing him to pieces was by plying them with tuns of wine at her funeral.

Although James was reported 'very sad' at Elizabeth's death, and promised his wife he would never again flaunt his mistress in public, he regained his good humour quickly enough to start an affair with Arabella Churchill, the daughter of Sir Winston Churchill, a keen royalist and Member of Parliament. Arabella first met James whilst out hunting in 1669; she fell off her horse, revealing a fine pair of legs. They were her best feature, for a contemporary described Arabella as 'a tall creature, pale faced, and nothing but skin and bone'.[42] Over the next decade they had five children. The first, James Fitzjames, became the Duke of Berwick and distinguished himself as a general in French service. Through her liaison Arabella was able to advance the career of her brother, John Churchill, Duke of Marlborough.

While James seemed to like all sorts of women, fair, dark, intelligent, Protestant and Catholic, he insisted they be young. Once they started to age he traded them in. Thus in 1678 he ditched Arabella for the young and beautiful Catherine Sedley.

Born the daughter of Sir Charles Sedley, a Kentish country gentleman, whose many infidelities made his wife so distraught that she had to be incarcerated in a nunnery (where she insisted that as Queen of England she be addressed as 'Your Majesty'), Catherine soon developed a reputation for eccentric promiscuity. Evelyn thought that at the age of fifteen she made up with wit what she obviously

15 *Arabella Churchill*, 'a tall creature, pale faced and nothing but skin and bone'. By Mary Beale (His Grace The Duke of Marlborough)

lacked in virtue. Three years later Sir Carr Scrope called her 'as mad as her mother and as vicious as her father'.[43]

James found her neither, particularly after she bore him a daughter, Catherine, in March 1679, and a son, James Darnley, in September 1684. But his second wife, Mary of Modena, whom he had married in 1674, was not so tolerant. She deeply resented her younger, and far more fecund rival. By the summer of 1680 the queen was reported 'very melancholy' about her husband's affairs: 'she prays almost everyday.'

Thus when James inherited the throne in 1685, Mary used her position as Queen of England to insist that her husband discharge his mistress, threatening that if he did not she would create a titanic scandal by becoming a nun. Many Protestants, including the Earl of Rochester, Anne Hyde's brother, supported Catherine Sedley as a counterweight to the Catholic queen. Catherine cited Magna Carta, which she claimed entitled her as a free-born Englishwoman to sleep with her king. The bribe of a house worth £10,000 and a pension of £4,000 a year managed to persuade Catherine that such might not have been one of King John and the Barons' intentions, and she left London for Dublin. Catherine hated Ireland and all its inhabitants, telling friends, 'I find them not only a senseless but a melancholy sort of people.' But when she returned to London the following year to regain her position, it was too late, for after fifteen years of vainly trying, Mary at last produced a son and heir. And thus she saved her marriage, while losing her husband his throne.

Since they knew that the boy would be brought up a Catholic, and that James's eldest daughter, Mary, the staunchly Protestant wife of William of Orange, would no longer inherit the throne and save England from Rome, several Whig aristocrats invited the couple to take over the kingdom, and thus precipitated the Revolution of 1688.

Before the Revolution James's mistresses had very little direct political influence. Even though Arabella Churchill and Catherine Sedley were staunch Protestants, they could do nothing to mitigate the king's rabid papism. When Elizabeth Denham tried to interfere in matters of state, James told her to mind her own business. As Pepys, who had known James when he was married to Anne Hyde fairly well, bluntly put it, 'The Duke of York in all things but his codpiece is led by his wife.'[44] But in one direct, but very important fashion his sexuality might well have affected his behaviour in middle age after he came to the throne.

As a young man James had amply demonstrated his courage. He

fought bravely in both French and Spanish service, at the battles of the Faubourg St Antoine and Dunkirk. As a British admiral he had two flagships sunk under him during the Battle of Sole Bay. Thus his craven reaction to William of Orange's invasion in 1688 requires some explanation. After moving his army southwest to Salisbury to meet the Dutch threat, James stayed in his room, debilitated by nose-bleeds, unable to sleep. At a council of war held on 22 November, the king urged an immediate retreat. It got underway two days later in great confusion, with James rushing hither and thither like some demented corporal, ordering, counter-ordering and disordering. On the 24th he left Salisbury for London, and after rejecting a constitutional settlement (similar to the one his father had turned down in 1641, which prompted the civil war), fled the capital on 19 December, throwing the Great Seal into the Thames. Recaptured, he was allowed to escape once again, this time reaching France on Christmas Day 1688.

The refusal of this war hero to fight, even for the Catholic cause which he valued above all others, was crucial. It helped make the Revolution of 1688 as 'Bloodless' as it was Glorious, and saved England (at least) from the horrors of the 1640s. In exile James turned his back on promiscuity, becoming instead morbidly religious. He used to visit the monks at La Trapp, an excessively gloomy bunch, who spent their days dressed in winding sheets, contemplating open graves, their silence being relieved only by the greeting, 'we must die brothers, we must die'. 'These are the only people I envy', the ex-king admitted before he died in 1701 from a stroke. His last words to his wife were: 'I am going to be happy.'[45]

On several occasions during his exile James hinted at the reasons for his failure to stand and fight in 1688. The repentant roué, who had once answered Bishop Burnet's criticisms of his philandering affairs with the retort 'If a man is religious need he become a saint?' now advised his son, 'Nothing has been more fatal to men, and to great men, than the letting themselves go in the forbidden love of Women.'[46] Again he told his heir 'I abhor and detest myself for having . . . lived so many years in almost a perpetual course of sin.' Might not James have been hinting that his real reason for doing nothing in 1688 was an almost unconscious desire to punish himself for what he described as his 'predominant sin'? Indeed might there be as much insight as there was cruelty to Charles II's jibe that the only reason why his younger brother's mistresses were all so ugly was that they 'were given to him by his priests by way of penance'?[47]

VI

'THE FROGS IN THE FABLE'

'No women ever came amiss to him', observed Lord Chesterfield about George I's mistresses, 'if they were very willing and very fat'. The eighteenth-century court wit and gossip went on to describe the best way to inveigle the king. 'The standards of His Majesty's taste made all those ladies who aspired to his favour, and who were of suitable size, strain and swell themselves like the frogs in the fable to rival the bulk and dignity of the ox. Some succeeded, and others burst.'[1]

Ever since then Englishmen have certainly found the king's German mistresses at best amusing, and at worst grotesque. There was Ehrengard Melusine Von Der Schulemburg – a woman whose physique somehow matched the magic of her name. She was so tall and so thin that English courtiers nicknamed her 'the maypole'. In contrast Sophia Charlotte, Frein Von Kielmannsegge, was so fat that she was known as 'the elephant'. This view of a Laurel and Hardy of torpidly tedious teutonic eroticism, has passed into folktales as typical of the foreigners who ruled England for roughly a century after the Glorious Revolution. They were fat, they weren't English, they didn't even speak the language, and by dallying with their ridiculous mistresses they somehow gave true Englishmen the opportunity of laying the foundations for political stability and parliamentary government.

As far as mistresses were concerned, however, the popular view of George I's (and George II's) paramours could not have been more wrong. Rather than diverting the German monarch from his job, they provided links between him and his English ministers that enabled those who learned the right techniques to maintain parliamentary support through the use of patronage and, at the same time, to retain the confidence of the crown as well. As Sir

Robert Walpole, England's first Prime Minister, who first achieved both goals, observed 'Nobody can carry on the king's business if he is not supported at Court.'[2]

In addition to changing the religious and constitutional face of England, the Revolution of 1688 altered the nature of court life drastically. Three of the next four monarchs were foreigners, who were as much, if not more interested in their native lands than their adopted kingdom. They spent as much time abroad as possible. At court they preferred the company of foreign advisers. However, by law they had to select British citizens as their ministers, and thus tended to use their mistresses as links between those they trusted and those on whom they were forced to rely.

William III, for instance, greatly preferred the company of his fellow Dutchmen. His main reason for accepting the crown of England was to use its resources to protect the Netherlands from French aggression. He was born in 1650, eight days after his father, the Dutch Stadtholder, had died of smallpox. Since his mother, Mary, Charles I's daughter, passed away when he was only ten, William had a lonely and restricted childhood. An English governess raised him; tutors educated him alone in the university city of Leiden.

During this childhood William's only real friend was his page, William Bentinck, the scion of a wealthy aristocratic family, who was utterly devoted to the prince. It was said that when William fell dangerously ill with smallpox, Bentinck slept in the same bed, in the belief that doing so would cure the patient by drawing the sickness out of him. On his recovery William was most grateful. 'I am so much your friend that I feel all that happens to you as if it had happened to myself', he wrote in 1665, to console Bentinck on the death of his father, adding 'I will seek any place and any occasion to show you effectively how much I can be your affectionate friend'.[3]

Not surprisingly, people started to speculate about the nature of their relationship. The French and Jacobites in particular encouraged the story that William was a homosexual. Dean Jonathan Swift (who years after William's death became the good friend of his mistress, Elizabeth Villiers) alleged that this was the case. Some have interpreted Bishop Burnet's statement that 'he had no vice but one sort, in which he was very cautious and secret',[4] to support this conclusion. It seems more likely, however, that the bishop, an intimate of the king, was referring to his long-standing affair with Elizabeth Villiers. William's standard modern biographer has vehemently denied the charges, asserting that 'the king's tremendous burden of work left no time for it'.[5]

William lacked libido more than he lacked time. A veteran soldier, he preferred the bonhomie of the campfire to the rustle of the boudoir. Before his marriage there was only one rumour of an affair (with an inn-keeper's daughter). It did not amount to much, since William's first priority was restoring the fortunes of the House of Orange.

After the English defeated the Dutch in 1654, John de Witt, the chief minister of the province of Holland, stripped the young William of the offices that the Orange family traditionally held. Even though he was only four at the time, the humiliation hurt William greatly. He determined on revenge. The opportunity came in 1672. After the French invaded Holland, there was a popular uprising against de Witt, who was murdered. Appointed Stadtholder of the Netherlands, and Captain General of her armed forces, William managed to halt the French advance. Thus he married Mary in 1677 mainly to form an English alliance to forestall Louis XIV.

Mary was the daughter of James II by his first wife, Anne Hyde, who had died when she was only nine. Two years later her father married Mary of Modena. In everything but religion she became very close to her father and his second wife, who was only four years her senior. Even after James II openly admitted that he had gone over to Rome, Mary remained a firm member of the Church of England. 'What ever happens', she wrote, 'I hope that my sister and I will keep our fidelity to God and our religion unblemished.'

A governess, Lady Frances Villiers, brought Mary up, together with her sister Anne. Both developed a deep friendship with Frances Apsely, a women nine years older than Mary, to whom she released her pent-up affections in long passionate letters. She called Frances 'her husband', and described herself as 'your humble servant to kiss the ground where you go, to be your dog on a string'.[6] While such gushing might seem embarrassing – even unhealthy – to modern ears, it reflected the intensity of an adolescent, reared on sentimental romances, who desperately wanted someone to love.

Unfortunately, the man Mary married was not such a person. After marrying William of Orange in 1677, and moving to Holland, Mary quickly fell in love with her husband and his country.

She did all she could to please him. Although William responded as best he could, Mary was too immature to provide the witty, cerebral companionship that he demanded of his intimates.

Such the Stadtholder found in the company of Elizabeth Villiers. A member of the celebrated family whose fortunes had been founded by George, Duke of Buckingham, three quarters of a century before, Elizabeth was no great beauty. She was ungainly, had a passable figure, and a long white neck. Dean Swift recalled that 'the good lady squints like a dragon'.[7] But as an old woman, at least, she had intelligence and wit enough to keep Swift up all night laughing, and as a young one the personality to ensnare William of Orange.

Elizabeth first came to Holland in 1677 as part of Mary's household. Almost immediately she attracted William's advances, which she tried to dissuade by encouraging those of Captain Wauchop, a Scots mercenary in Dutch employ. William dismissed his rival. Elizabeth soon succumbed: rumours of an affair were rife in Paris by the summer of 1679.

When his wife learned about the liaison the following year she was distraught. Mary fell ill: she seemed to lose the will to live. Eventually she came to accept that such arrangements were a common enough princely prerogative. They could hardly come as a surprise to James II's daughter, and Charles II's niece. So for some years William and Mary's marriage jogged along, as they tried in vain to conceive a child.

Soon after coming to the English throne in 1685 James II tried to use William's affair with Elizabeth Villiers to discredit his son-in-law, and possibly destroy his daughter's marriage. Such would dash the Dutchman's hopes of ever using England to further the Protestant cause. Dr Covell, Mary's chaplain, and Mrs Trelawney, her old nanny, informed Bevil Skelton, the British Ambassador to the Netherlands, about the liaison. He formally brought it to Mary's attention. Humiliated by this public – and rather undiplomatic – rebuke Mary stationed herself early one morning outside Elizabeth Villier's apartments: at two o'clock she surprised her husband. He became so angry, and Mary so tearful that the couple could not bear each other's company for several days.

Even though the Stadtholder eventually promised his wife that in future he would be faithful and agreed to dismiss Elizabeth (who actually returned to England for a short while), the main casualty of the incident was not William and Mary's marriage, but

16 *Elizabeth Villiers*, mistress of William of Orange. Undated portrait by Sir Peter Lely (From the collection of the Earl of Jersey)

their relations with James II. Outraged to discover that Covell was telling his father-in-law that at the Dutch court 'none but pimps and bawds must expect tolerable usage',[8] William dismissed the chaplain, and insisted that James recall the British ambassador. Mary did what she could to keep her new-won love. As her father became more and more unpopular, she let the Whig grandees know that she was willing to go along with their plans to replace him with William, and that she was quite happy to be joint ruler with her husband, whom she would – like any god-fearing seventeenth-century wife – obey. Ultimately Mary was prepared to break the fifth commandment in the hope that it would prevent her husband from breaching the seventh.

It did not work. Elizabeth soon returned, and Mary had to put up with her husband's infidelities. In 1690 it was reported that their marriage was breaking up, since Elizabeth was pregnant with William's child. Fortunately their marriage survived the crisis, for if it had not then the revolutionary settlement would have surely collapsed with it.

When Mary died of smallpox three years later on 28 December 1694, William was far more upset than most people who knew the state of his marriage would have anticipated. Just before she died Mary burnt most of her private letters, and wrote one to her husband, to be opened after she had passed away, begging him to dismiss Elizabeth Villiers for the sake of his immortal soul. Promising Archbishop Tenison 'I must mend my life', William never again saw Elizabeth in public. Instead he gave her lands worth £30,000 a year, and married her off to George Hamilton, the Earl of Orkney, a brave soldier with a stutter, and little to say for himself.

William never remarried. Instead he preferred the company of Arnold Joost Van Keppel, a Dutch lad who had come to England as a page boy, and (like Robert Carr) attracted the king's attention when he fell from his horse and broke a leg. Bentinck, who resented losing influence to the younger man, warned the king about the gossip engendered by his intimacy with Keppel (whom he elevated Earl of Portland). Irate, William retorted 'It is a most extraordinary thing that one could have no esteem or friendship for a young man without its being criminal.'[9] In fact William felt towards Keppel as he would have to the son that Mary had never given him. Indeed, as his infidelities suggest, what William wanted from a woman was wit and conversation. All he needed from a wife was a political connection that would protect his beloved Holland. From neither companion did he much value sex. And judged by that criterion William and Mary's marriage was a success.

The relationship between William's successor, Queen Anne, Sarah Churchill, and her husband John, Duke of Malborough, was of profound importance in English history. By providing a link between the crown and Britain's leading general, it helped the nation win the War of Spanish Succession, and between 1702 and 1707 brought the Whigs a political prominence which they lost to the Tories when Abigail Masham displaced Sarah as the queen's favourite.

At the time many a tongue wagged about the exact nature of the queen's feelings. After all, her husband, George of Denmark, was such a nonentity that Charles II had to confess, 'I've tried him drunk and I've tried him sober, but there's nothing to him'.[10] George made Anne pregnant at least seventeen times, but none of their children survived to adulthood. Perhaps Anne resented men since they caused her so much pain and grief. Certainly she felt an uneasy passion towards other women. Like her elder sister Mary, as a teenager Anne used to write to Frances Apsely in terms of cloying affection. Sarah recalled that her friend 'used to say that she desired her wholly'.[11] But it would be wrong to agree with the modern author who has described their friendship 'as a typical lesbian relationship', or with the contemporary broadsheets which argued that Sarah owed her influence over the queen to 'some dark Deed at night'.[12] Theirs was the attraction of opposites: Sarah was beautiful, witty, self-confident, and charming, the centre of attention; Anne was plain, shy, insecure, desperate for some one with whom she could be an equal and from whom she could expect absolute honesty, if not utter loyalty. Sarah was too much in love with her husband, whom she fondly recalled would on returning from campaigning immediately 'pleasure her with his boots on',[13] to be bisexual. More convincingly, a month after Sarah accused her rival Abigail Masham of 'having no inclination for any but of one's own sex', Anne broke with Sarah, and never forgave the slur.[14]

With the accession of the Hanoverians in 1714, royal promiscuity became more open, albeit more ridiculous, if only because there was a male once again on the throne, and because a generation after the Revolution of 1688 the political order had grown stable enough to tolerate a scandal. Indeed it was to erode this stability that the supporters of Charles Stuart, the Young Pretender, spread sinister stories about the Elector of Hanover's wife and mistresses even before George I succeeded to the British throne.

Born in 1660, George first came to England when he was twenty to propose to Anne, James, Duke of York's daughter by his wife, Anne Hyde. Prince Rupert, Charles I's great general, as well as his nephew, urged the union. Since George's mother, Sophia, did not approve of her eldest son making an alliance with a commoner's daughter, the Earl of Clarendon's lineage being, she felt 'une family fort mediocre', negotiations got nowhere. Anyway, Anne had the last laugh: she became Queen of England, and by outliving Sophia by two months prevented her from inheriting the throne. So in November 1682 George had to cut his marital cloth to fit a German princeling's coat, by settling for the Duke of Lüneburg-Celle's daughter, Sophia Dorothea.

Although the young couple did not wed as reluctantly as many have supposed, Sophia Dorothea was too immature, too spoilt, and too lacking in self-discipline to make a success of their union, particularly as her husband was often away fighting the Turks in the service of the Holy Roman Empire. They had their first child, George August (later George II of England), in December 1683, and their second, Sophia Dorothea, in 1687. By then their marriage was on the rocks. Bored, lonely, unable to make friends in Hanover, Sophia Dorothea expressed her anger in tantrums, particularly after her husband started an affair. Fatally, she decided to follow suit.

Philip Christoph von Konigsmarck was a Swedish Count, who had been a colonel in the Hanoverian army since 1689. He was good looking, and high spirited, and since his sister was married to an officer in the Duke of Lüneburg-Celle's service, provided Sophia Dorothea with both a link to her family and an amusing diversion. In 1690 she allowed him to start writing to her. After a brief pause she began to reply. They had secret meetings, and by March 1692 their letters reveal that they were lovers. 'What joy, what pleasure, what enchantment have I not felt in your arms. God! What a night I have spent!' Konigsmarck wrote to his mistress. 'I was born to love you and be eternally yours', she replied, 'I would give half my blood to hold you in my arms.'[15]

Foolish with passion, both of them were under the misapprehension that the intensity of their affections precluded any need for prudence or discretion.

Neither went unwarned of the dangers of their behaviour. Sophia Dorothea's mother told her that the affair must end. Konigsmarck's brother officers advised him that he was playing with fire. When his commander in chief interviewed him, Konigsmarck replied that there was 'nothing to it'. As the scandal grew, so too did the lovers' recklessness: they took full and virtually open advantage of George's absence first on a military campaign and then on a diplomatic mission to Berlin, to seal their fate. When Konisgsmarck came to Hanover in the summer of 1684 he carried on with a blatancy that seemed to confirm the rumours that he and Sophia Dorothea were about to elope.

During the night of 1 July the Swedish Count was reported entering the palace, and making his way to Sophia Dorothea's apartments. He was never seen again – dead or alive. It was rumoured that the Countess Von Platen, *maîtresse en titre* to George's father, Ernest Augustus, had lured him to his death. Almost certainly he was murdered by a group of five courtiers, who dumped Konigsmarck's body in the Liene River in a sack weighted with stones. It is not known whether they did so on their own initiative or on orders from the jealous husband.

George acted quickly. He ordered a search of Sophia Dorothea's rooms that found incriminating letters from Konigsmarck. In December he obtained a divorce from his wife on the grounds not of her adultery – for such would have been too humiliating – but because of her refusal to cohabit. Sophia Dorothea initially welcomed the divorce proceedings in the misapprehension that they would free her to remarry Konigsmarck, whom she still believed alive. But when her husband and father agreed that she should be kept in virtual house arrest in Ahlen Castle, Sophia Dorothea felt betrayed. Even though the conditions of her imprisonment were not as onerous as George's enemies alleged, she remained restricted until her death in 1726, a bitter, ageing woman, determined to clear her name, and denied the right to see her children, who anyway sided with their father. In sum she was a clear example of the sexual double standard of royalty.

The divorce hurt George deeply. His wife's infidelities, and her unfavorable comments in her letters to Konigsmarck about his abilities in bed stung him to the quick. The affair also taught him to keep his own counsel, to watch out for intrigues by those whom he trusted, and to secure the goals set for him by his parents. Ironically the divorce helped make George a more effective ruler and a better king of Britain than many have credited. It also made him treasure the secure, morganatic relationship he developed with his mistress Ehrengard Melusine Von Der Schulemburg, the woman who helped break up his marriage in the first place.

None the less the prevailing image of George I is of a boorishly incompetent German, with 'a healthy appetite for women', whom 'he preferred fat and complacent', and who were tributes to 'the King's bad taste and strong stomach'. Typical of such dyspeptic ladies was Sophia Charlotte Kielmansegge. Horace Walpole recorded meeting her as a child and 'being terrified of her enormous figure, the fierce black eyes, large and rolling between two lofty arched eyebrows, two acres of cheeks spread with crimson, an ocean of neck that overflowed and was not distinguished from the lower part of her body'.[16]

To the sins of boundless flesh, contemporaries added charges of incest. It was widely believed that Sophia Charlotte was George's illegitimate half-sister by the Countess Von Platen. Apologists have countered that the countess was so promiscuous that the odds that George's father was the lover to sire Sophia Charlotte were remote. Anyway the question was moot for the relationship between George I and Sophia Charlotte amounted to little more than the mutual and platonic enjoyment of her wit and his money.

The king's real mistress, Ehrengard Melusine Von Der Schulemburg has received just as bad, and as unfair, a press. The Electress Sophia called Melusine a scarecrow, and a hop-pole, adding 'You would scarcely believe that she has captivated my son.'[17] Lady Mary Wortley Montagu observed that the attraction between the king and Melusine was that of like minds: 'She was duller than himself and consequently did not find out that was so.'[18] Sir Robert Walpole, that expert on everyone's price, thought that she 'would have sold the king's honour for a shilling advanced to the highest bidder'. He added that her intellect was 'mean and contemptible'.[19]

Be that as it may, at least Melusine had a pleasant face and a kindly nature. She was a patient woman, with sense enough to respond to George's wishes. She learned both to share his taste in music, and how to manage his moods. They had three daughters, the first, Anna Louise, being born in 1682. Even though by 1698 Melusine was generally recognized as George's *maîtresse en titre*, who acted as hostess for formal entertainments, and was accorded the appropriate precedence, the king never acknowledged the girls' paternity: doing so would have prejudiced the validity of his divorce. None the less he was deeply fond of his daughters, who with their mother became the real 'family' that gave him the domestic stability he could never hope to find with his legitimate children or his divorced and disgraced wife. Gertrude, his youngest daughter by Melusine, was a noted beauty, of whom the king was especially fond. She used to read the newspapers out aloud to him and would accompany him hunting. So stable, then, were George's relations with Melusine and her children, that Walpole observed that she was 'in effect, as much Queen of England as any ever was: that he did everything by her'.[20]

Not surprisingly, it took Melusine some time to adjust to George's elevation from Hanover to England. When she first came to London it seemed to many that her main concerns were collecting money and titles. She was extremely angry that the best that Secretary of State Charles Townsend could do was to have her made Duchess of Munster, a mere Irish peerage. So she schemed to have Townsend made Lord Lieutenant of Ireland, damaging his influence at court, as well as that of his ally, Sir Robert Walpole. Their rivals, Charles Spencer, Earl of Sunderland, and Lord James Stanhope, managed to ingratiate themselves with the king's mistress – and thus the king – by having Melusine made Duchess of Kendal a particularly prestigious title whose royal connections went back to 1389.

Such a public demonstration of clout prompted many to bribe Melusine and Sophia Charlotte. For instance, during the first five years of the reign, James Brydges, the ambitious Duke of Chandos, gave each of them over £9,500. Greed appeared to be chief characteristic of these two ladies, both of whom were believed to have made a speculative killing from the South Sea Bubble.

The collapse of the South Sea Bubble in 1720 proved to be a turning point in George I's reign. It destroyed Spencer and Stanhope's influence, leaving a political vacuum which Townsend and Walpole filled. They gained the thanks of Melusine and Sophia Charlotte for covering up their part in scandal. Melusine tried to sweep the matter under the rug by using her influence to prevent the extradition of an official of the South Sea Company back to England, where he might implicate those close to the king. She was not yet completely committed to the new ministry, still retaining a soft spot for Spencer (who luckily for Walpole died in 1722). A little later in return for a £10,000 bribe she persuaded the king to pardon Henry St John, Viscount Bolingbroke, the Tory politician, whom he had dismissed a decade earlier.

But Melusine recognized that in matters of moment she had no hope of circumventing Townsend and Walpole, who were able to prevent Bolingbroke from regaining his once considerable powers. So she had sense enough to work with them to help create a stable and strong administration. One Prussian diplomat recognized that often it was Melusine who 'broke the first ice with the king'. As Townsend confessed to Walpole frequently she 'strained her interest, perhaps further than was advisable with the king to help them'.[21] In return they did all they could to keep Sophie Karoline, the Countess Von Platen from joining the king in England. The countess's youth and looks made her a dangerous threat to Melusine's position, while her alliance with Lord John Carteret jeopardized that of Townsend and Walpole.

Neither need have worried, for during the 1720s their power grew. In 1719, for instance, a French diplomatic report on English politics did not mention Melusine. Five years later the ambassador advised Louis XV that 'nothing can be more conducive to my interests' than 'to acquire a share of her confidence'.

Towards the end of the reign Melusine was secure enough even to survive a royal dalliance with a younger woman, Anne Brent, the Countess of Macclesfield's daughter. Anne had fine black hair, and such dark skin that she became known as 'the Sultana'. Many took her to be a Spaniard, but she was an Englishwoman, a sign, perhaps that the Hanoverian king was coming to terms with his adopted land. She never managed to have any political influence with George I, perhaps because, as one courtier put it, insolence was 'the chief characteristic of the new Sultana'.

For this reason Melusine never worried that Anne might displace her. She was far more interested in making money than in constitutional or diplomatic developments, and preferred Townsend over Walpole. But there is no doubt that in doing so she helped establish and maintain the latter's strong and stable administration which has been widely recognized as that of Britain's first Prime Minister.

George I died on 11 June 1727 while he was journeying home to his beloved Hanover. He passed away in Osnabrück, in the very same room in which he happened to be born.[22] Melusine was distraught. It was said that 'she beat her breast, she tore her hair'.[23] Soon afterward Melusine returned to England, where she lived until her own death in 1746. According to one story she missed her lover so much that she came to believe that George had come back to her in the form of a bird, whom she befriended with crumbs, and eventually tamed.

For Walpole the first George's death presented political rather than emotional adjustments. Now he had to befriend and tame a new king who had hated the old.

If there was one constant amongst the Hanoverians as a family it was a deep and consistent hatred between fathers and sons.

For instance, George II openly alleged that Sophia Charlotte had slept with every man in Hanover. Far from dismissing this ridiculous charge – for Hanover was far from a small electorate, that was populated by particularly earnest Protestants and anyway Sophia Charlotte's weight precluded such a marathon – the wronged woman had her husband sign a certificate attesting to her fidelity. 'It is a very bad reputation, Madame', noted the heir's wife, Princess Caroline, 'which needs such support'. One court lady added that it must have been the first such certificate ever issued.

A few years later George I quarrelled publicly with the future George II at the christening of his first son. The king was convinced that his heir had impugned the Duke of Newcastle's honour, and might even have challenged him to a duel. After placing his son under close arrest, George I expelled him and his wife from the palace, while retaining control of their children – as English law allowed.

George II and his wife Caroline were on equally malevolent terms with their heir, Frederick, Prince of Wales. The king once described him as 'a monster and the greatest villain that was ever born'. His mother remarked that if she ever saw him burning in hell 'I should feel not more for him that I would feel for any other rogue that went there'. Without a shred of evidence, she was convinced that her eldest son was impotent, and that he was such a blaggard that he had another man father his purported children.[24]

Unscrupulous politicians – and in eighteenth-century England there were few who were not – naturally took advantage of such family feuds. The 'outs' clustered around the heir in the hope that when the monarch died they would become the 'ins'. Of course such was a dangerous ploy, that appealed only to those who had scant chance of getting power in the normal course of political events. Thus those who advised the king's eldest sons were often men whose desperation for office was exceeded only by their ambitions.

Walpole recognized this dilemma long before George I died, and used his influence with Caroline to build a flyover to the new king that bypassed his old friends. The Norfolk squire justified his decision to rely on the queen rather than a mistress to control the king with a simile that his fellow country gentleman, such as Fielding's Squire Weston, would have readily appreciated: 'he took', he said, 'the right sow by the ear.' In doing so he reversed the situation that had existed during the old reign: Caroline took over Melusine's political role as a conduit between the monarch and his first minister.

That does not mean that George II was utterly uxorious. For instance he enjoyed an affair with Mrs Henrietta Howard for well over a decade. She was the daughter of a Norfolk squire whose large family had diluted her expectations. As a young woman Henrietta married Charles Howard, the Earl of Suffolk's younger son and a wastrel whom Lord Hervey described as 'wrong headed, ill-tempered, obstinate, drunken, extravagant, brutal'.[25] But at least he had enough sense to go over to Hanover to try to mend his fortunes in the service of the heir to the English throne. At first Charles and Henrietta were so poor that she had to sell tresses of her fine, light brown hair. Soon she found an easier way to turn a penny.

Charles Howard – who on the basis of his wife's exertions was promoted Groom of the Bedchamber – was far from pleased by her success. He ordered Henrietta to return to her conjugal duties, and even obtained a writ from the Lord Chief Justice authorizing him to seize his wife. The cuckold went to plead his case with Caroline, and became so angry that she was afraid that he might throw her out of the window. Only the grant of a pension worth £1,200 a year managed to cure his ill-humour (as well as his immediate financial problems) and allowed George to continue to enjoy his love.

By no stretch of the imagination was Henrietta a beauty. Fleshy, she had a nice nature, with a plain, yet pleasing face. Even her enemies agreed that 'she was civil to everybody, friendly to many, and unjust to none. In short she had a good head and a good heart.'[26] While Henrietta was no blue-stocking she was intelligent

17 *Henrietta Howard*, Countess of Suffolk and mistress of George II. 'Civil to every-body, friendly to many and unjust to none.' By John Harris after Michael Dahl (National Portrait Gallery)

enough to win the respect of savants such as Jonathan Swift and Alexander Pope. The latter wrote of her:

> *I know a thing that's most uncommon.*
> *(Envy be silent and attend!)*
> *I know a remarkable woman,*
> *Handsome and witty, yet a friend.*
>
> *Not warped by passion, aw'd by rumour,*
> *Not grave through pride, or gay through folly,*
> *And an equal mixture of good humour,*
> *And sensible soft melancholy.*[27]

Every evening at nine, as regular as clockwork, the king would go to Henrietta's apartments where he would stay for several hours. Horace Walpole disillusioned the naive who wondered if they might be passing their hours in erudite conversation, by observing that she was so deaf and his 'passions were so indelicate' that they could not rise to platonic pleasures. The king's gift to Henrietta of a pension of £2,000 a year substantiated Walpole's cynicism.

But that was practically all she got out of George II. Being the royal mistress was, one courtier noted, about as regular, exciting, and physically challenging as being a mill horse plodding around its constant track. As far as long-term royal mistresses go, Henrietta was most likely the least well rewarded. A pension, a villa outside London, a few trinkets, and the privilege of helping comb the queen's hair (as Caroline nagged her Lady of the Bedchamber to do it properly) were all Henrietta got from over a decade's service to the crown.

No wonder in 1734 she decided to leave the king, much to Caroline's chagrin, for the queen felt that having Henrietta as a rival was no threat at all. Hearing of his wife's efforts to persuade his mistress to remain, George reprimanded Caroline, 'What the devil did you mean by trying to make an old, dull, deaf, peevish beast stay and plague me.'[28]

George II handled the matter with the chivalry that characterized all his dealings with the fair sex. For instance, a few years earlier Mary Bellenden had caught the royal eye at a court ball. According to Lord Hervey she was 'incontestable the most agreeable, the most insinuating, and the most likeable woman of her time'.[29] 'Smiling Mary, soft and fair as down',[30] was the composer John Gay's description. So that randy old stag, George II, plonked himself on a settee next to her, ogled her without restraint, and over and over again counted out the gold in his purse as if he contemplated making an offer. 'Sir, I can bear it no longer. If you count your money once more I shall leave the room', declared the frightened young woman. He did. So suddenly kicking the money, sending the coins flying, she fled the room, and married the future Duke of Argyll. She lived in the depths of the countryside, safe from crude royal advances.

After Henrietta bolted from the court George II wasted no time finding a replacement. He had a brief affair with Lady Deloraine, a drunken little slut whose promiscuity was pronounced enough to provoke adverse comment even amongst the worldly court gossips of her day. Sir Robert Walpole (who was always anxious about losing the royal favour) complained to Lord Hervey that he wished that George II had not chosen to sleep with such a mischievous little bitch. Hervey reassured him that, 'If she got the ear of anyone in power, it might be of a very bad consequence, but since 'tis only the king I think it of no great significance.'[31] But as was so often the case, Hervey allowed his wit (and perhaps hindsight) to overrule his political judgement, for the choice of a royal mistress was still a matter of moment.

In 1735 on a trip to Hanover George fell in love with Amelia Sophia von Walmoden, a married woman twenty-one years his junior. 'She has fine black eyes, and brown hair, and very well shaped', wrote an observer, 'not tall nor low, has no fine features, but very agreeable in the main. It is not doubted that she will soon have an apartment at Kensington.'[32] George pursued the young lady with his usual energy and finesse, describing every move in forty- to fifty-page letters to his wife back in England. She was young, beautiful, fashionable, and extremely accommodating, wrote the king, before ingenuously reassuring the queen 'I know you will love Madame Walmoden, because she loves me'.[33]

The main political effect of this liaison was to exacerbate George's dislike of England and increase his regard for Hanover. Forced to return to London late in the year he arrived back in a foul mood (worsened by an attack of piles brought on by riding virtually non-stop). Promptly he had a fight with his wife. The following year he went back to Hanover to see Madame Walmoden and their son. The king's absences abroad made him extremely unpopular in England. One wag pushed an old, broken-down nag out to wander about the streets of London with a note around its head: 'I am the King's

Hanoverian Equipage going to fetch his Majesty and his whore to England.'[34]

According to Lord Hervey (who knew the king as well as he disliked him), such jibes amused George II. He saw them as tributes to his virility. As Hervey perceptively realized, the king had to 'have some woman for the world to believe that he lay with her'.[35] Caroline, who was much more intelligent than her spouse, tolerated this situation because she realized that a contented husband was also a pliant one. At times it seemed as if, for George, adultery was a royal public duty and marriage the true secret pleasure. With his mistresses he was punctual in his obligations, visiting Mrs Howard every night at nine. To his wife he was the romantic, for he recognized that ultimately she was the love of his life, whom as both man and monarch he needed more than anyone else.

Such Caroline's death painfully brought home to the king. For several years she had suffered from stomach cancer. In November 1737 her diseased innards burst, spilling the putrefaction all over the place. Alexander Pope, a friend of Henrietta, maliciously observed:

> Here lies, wrapped in forty thousand towels,
> The only proof that Caroline had bowels.[36]

The queen bore her sufferings with her usual fortitude, and without anaesthetics. As he was probing her stomach with his knife one surgeon leaned so far forward that he bumped into a candle, setting fire to his wig. Caroline asked for the operation to be suspended for a few moments so she could laugh without literally busting her already strained gut.

Desperately upset, George went to see his dying wife. He assured her that he could never love another woman as he had loved her. He would never take another wife. No! I will only take a mistress, he promised his wife. My God, if only I could believe it, replied the dying queen.

The king in fact kept his promise. After Caroline passed away, he summoned Lady Deloraine back to his bed, but soon dismissed her because, as he explained, she smelt of cheap Spanish wine.

Madame Walmoden returned from Hanover, to become the king's loyal companion for the rest of his life. She divorced her husband in 1739, and the following year George made her Duchess of Yarmouth. At first her political influence was slight, being confined mainly to arranging the sale of peerages to all-comers, including the son of a Barbados peddler, and a footman's grandson. But over the years her power grew. She did much to persuade George II to let Pitt take over the government during the military crisis of 1756. By acting as a conduit between the king and his prickly prime minister, Madame Walmoden helped Pitt win the Seven Years War. She had sense enough to dissuade George from dismissing Pitt, bravely telling the angry monarch that doing so would bring back the political chaos that had preceded the present administration.

The private limits of Madame Walmoden's influence became public after George II died in 1760. In his will the king ordered that he be buried in St George's Chapel, Windsor, in the crypt next to Caroline, and that the adjacent sides of their specially designed coffins should be raised to allow their bodies to mingle once again. In death George II proved once more that the only mistress of his life was his wife.

The king's son and heir, Frederick, was far less constant. His father loathed him. His mother called him 'my half-witted coxcomb'. The public dubbed him 'Poor Fred'. Sir Robert Walpole described him as 'a poor, weak, irresolute, false, lying, dishonest, contemptible wretch, that nobody loves, that nobody believes, that nobody will trust'.[37] And his behaviour towards Anne Vane seemed to prove all of them right.

They became lovers during the latter part of 1730, even though Anne was also having affairs with Lords Harrington and Hervey, as well as, declared Queen Caroline, having 'lain with half the town'.[38] Apparently she made up with energy what she lacked in looks and stature, for a contemporary described her as 'a fat, ill-shaped dwarf'. The following June she gave birth to a son, which Frederick – with more pride than certainty – acknowledged as his own, having the boy christened Cornwall Fitzfrederick. Soon afterwards, tiring of the child's mother, he tried to pension Anne off with £1,500 a year, and a £20,000 settlement on marriage. But rather than accept this most generous offer, she sent the prince a pathetic letter complaining that she would not be cast aside 'after she sacrificed my time, my youth, my character, the world, my family, and everything a woman can sacrifice to the man she loves'.[39] Once this pathetic appeal became public knowledge Frederick's reputation sank even further, for many felt that he had not acted towards his ex-mistress like a gentleman. Thus while his sudden death in 1751 came as a shock, he was not mourned as much of a loss. During the later part of the eighteenth century England was changing drastically, and if the monarchy failed to alter with it, then royalty might well not survive.

VII
'THE DAMNEDEST MILLSTONES'

During the sixty-year reign of George III Great Britain changed profoundly. Between 1760 and 1820 the Industrial Revolution started, bringing about a new economic order that allowed Britain to dominate the western world for the next hundred years. The face of the landscape altered as fields were enclosed, commons were divided, and people moved from the rural south to the dark satanic mills of the North, the Midlands, South Wales and the Scottish Lowlands. A new professional middle class emerged, which demanded political power commensurate with its new economic wealth. When the established church became so complacent, and so indifferent to the needs of the new industrial working class, Methodism filled the void. Political bungling and insular arrogance helped lose the American Colonies, while the inspired leadership of men such as Nelson and Wellington contributed to victory in the Napoleonic Wars.

There was, too, a change in the ethical climate, particularly among the new entrepreneurial classes produced by the Industrial Revolution. To improve every aspect of peoples' lives they founded societies such as the Forlorn Females' Fund of Mercy, the Scripture Admonition Society, the Vice Society, the Society of Young Ladies to Sell Clothes at Reduced Prices, and the City of London Truss Society for the Relief of the Ruptured Poor throughout the Kingdom. They were even more chagrined about disjunctions amongst the rich. The easy promiscuity, flaunted by the aristocracy especially, that went back to the Restoration, became far less open. Gone were the days when the monthly magazine, *Town and Country*, ran a regular profile on some famous man's mistress. Euphemisms, such as 'gallantry' for 'adultery', that encouraged sexuality, were replaced with ones which denied it. Bitches became known as 'mother mastiffs'. London's

Codpiece Row was renamed Coppice Row. In 1802 the Reverend Bowdler gave his name to the language by producing a sanitized version of Shakespeare. Intolerance grew – or, if you prefer, there was an improvement in the moral tone. 'Where is male chastity to be found', bemoaned John Wesley, 'how few can lay any claim to it at all?'[1]

But not withstanding the best (or worst) efforts of both John Wesley and Thomas Bowdler, human nature did not alter all that much. If the new moral climate no longer condoned finding love outside marriage, then the elite realized that they had to find affection within that institution. Marriages for dynastic convenience became less common. Parents allowed their children more say in the choice of a mate, for, as Jane Austen warned, 'anything is to be professed or demurred rather than marriage without affection. Nothing can be compared with the misery of being bound without love.'[2]

The reasons for this change in moral tone are hard to find. Perhaps they were part of the reaction that seems inevitable in human affairs. Methodism, which began as a protest against the conplacency of the Anglican Church, stressed simple domestic virtues. Certainly the security of stable family life appealed to the new middle class. Some thought that Britain's defeat in the American Revolution was a punishment from the Almighty for being an aristocratic Sodom and Gomorrah. Later, others interpreted Britain's victory in the Napoleonic Wars as an equally sure sign of His approval. All agreed, however, that the domestic probity of the king's personal life accorded with the new moral tone.

For instance, George III, stopped holding Court dinners on Sundays so as to better observe the Lord's Day. Such probity was very different from the wickedness of his sons. Their debts, gambling, whoring, selfishness, and pure personal malice became so blatant that the Duke of Wellington described the king's sons as 'the damnedest millstones about the neck of any government that can be imagined'.[3]

Posterity has not treated George III kindly. The Declaration of Independence called him 'a Tyrant . . . unfit to be the Ruler of a Free people'. One eminent Victorian, W. E. H. Lecky, thought him 'Ignorant, arbitrary, and narrow-minded'. Yet during the second half of his reign, at least, no monarch was more popular than George III. In part, his esteem was due to a widespread sympathy for the illness – now diagnosed as porphyria, a genetic disease – which turned him into a sad, mad, Lear-like prisoner in Windsor Castle. But George also touched many of those themes which have enabled the modern constitutional monarchy to survive and flourish. For example, during his reign the sovereign became the symbol of British patriotism. 'God Save the King' was adopted as the National Anthem, being sung with much enthusiasm and great frequency whenever the king appeared in public. Soldiers used their swords to remove the hats of those who refused to stand bare-headed when it was performed. King George and Queen Charlotte managed to combine domestic ordinariness with majestic dignity in a way that ever since has been part of the royal family's mystique. 'The whole Nation . . . like one great family', exulted one newspaper during the king's Jubilee in 1807, united 'in solemn prayer and thanksgiving for . . . the Father of his People.'[4] This sentiment was repeated when George III died at the age of eighty-two in January 1820. 'And thus sunk into a honoured grave the best man and best king that ever adorned humanity', wrote Mrs Arbuthnot in her diary after attending his funeral, 'who for sixty long years had been the father to his people.'[5]

George was a far better father to his people than to his own children. He was utterly faithful to his wife – so much so that one historian has conjectured that it was the performance of his conjugal duties with 'a resolute fidelity to a hideous Queen' that helped engender his emotional problems![6] While that remains no more than speculation there is no doubt that the king's sense of duty produced a quiverful of children – nine sons and six daughters in all. When the children were young their parents treated them well. But they would not let them grow up. They kept them in baby clothes long after other children were allowed to graduate into adult dress, and as adolescents denied them the independence that their peers enjoyed.

The king and queen were particularly restrictive towards their six daughters. Only three of the girls ever married: Charlotte when she was thirty-one, Mary at forty, while poor Elizabeth had to wait until she was forty-eight. Being raised in what one of them recalled as a well run convent inflicted emotional scars on the royal daughters. The oldest, Charlotte, made an indifferent marriage to Frederick, Prince of Wurtemburg. He was so fat that Napoleon observed that the only reason why God could have possibly created him was to demonstrate how far human skin could stretch without breaking. It was widely rumoured that Princess Sophia had an illegitimate child by General Thomas Garth, a short man, thirty-three years her senior, with a birthmark on his forehead and one eye. Her father accepted the story that the dropsy had made her belly swell, and that 'the roast beef cure' had prompted its sudden contraction. At the age of seventeen the king's youngest daughter, Amelia, fell in love with General Charles Fitzroy, and after a decade of unrequited passion, died in 1807, leaving him the bulk of her estate.

While restrictive as a parent, as a husband George III was a moral paragon, particularly when compared to his relatives. His uncle, William Augustus, Duke of Cumberland (the notorious 'Butcher' of Culloden) enjoyed copulating with blowsey actresses. His youngest sister, Caroline Matilda, sought refuge from her marriage with Christian VII, the homosexual King of Denmark, and a diseased and demented debauchee, by having an affair with her physician. When Christian discovered he executed his wife's lover, and she might have suffered the same fate had not George III threatened to send the Royal Navy to bombard Copenhagen if he did not let her return home in disgrace.

The king's brothers were just as impulsive. Frederick, Duke of York, 'was silly, frivolous, and heartless', thought Lady Louisa Stuart, 'void alike of steadiness and principle; libertine in practice'.[7] William Henry, the Duke of Gloucester, secretly married Lady Maria Waldgrave, the illegitimate daughter of Edward Walpole (the Prime Minister's brother) and one Mrs Clements, a milliner. The fact that she was the widow of George III's childhood governor, whom the king remembered as 'a depraved worthless man',[8] did nothing to recommend the union. Neither did this wilful woman's ambitions: until their marriage collapsed in 1786, she forced her lackadaisical husband into scheming against the monarch.

George's youngest brother, Henry, Duke of Gloucester, caused the king even more grief. Henry shocked London society (which was in itself quite an achievement) by flaunting his mistresses as he drove them around Hyde Park in a coach bearing the royal coat of arms. Henry's preference for married ladies got him into legal hot water. In 1770 Lord Grosvenor sued him for adultery with his wife, and collected £10,000 damages (less for alienation of affections than for the unauthorized use of his Lordship's property). A year later George III – already annoyed by having to lend his brother the money to pay for Grosvenor's damages and court costs – discovered that Henry had secretly married Anne Horton, a widow, two years his senior. Exasperated he declared that his brother exhibited the morals of 'a Newgate Attorney', adding 'I now wash my hands of the affair and will have no further intercourse with him'.[9]

But, for the king, his brother's matings were not merely a matter of morality. Cognisant of the example of Edward IV's union with Elizabeth Woodville, George III was convinced that the mingling of royal with common blood would inevitably lead to a repeat of the Wars of the Roses. Thus in 1772 he had his Prime Minister, Lord North, introduce legislation into parliament prohibiting all members of the Royal Family from marrying without the sovereign's permission, without which all future marriages were null and void. Even though practically every member agreed with Edward Gibbon that this would be 'a most monstrous law', parliament caved in to royal pressure, and passed the Royal Marriage Act that rendered null and void all unions the king's offspring might make without his permission. As a result Lord North received the Order of the Garter, and George III's sons gained a *carte blanche* to fornicate without legal let or hindrance as wantonly as their self-indulgent appetites permitted, promising, and even entering into marriages, confident that their vows had no force in law.

Few men have spent so much time, money, and effort in indulging themselves as George IV. In 1812, when he was Prince Regent, the poet Leigh Hunt called him 'a libertine ever head over heels in debt and disgrace, a despiser of domestic ties'. For such candour Hunt was fined £500 and sentenced to two years in prison for libel.[10] Prince George's selfish dissipation could have started as an attempt to rebel against his parents' incessant nagging to 'Abhor all vice, in private as well as in public'.[11] Certainly George was convinced that 'the king hates me: he always did from seven years old'.[12]

At the age of sixteen Prince George continued what had become almost a royal tradition by losing his virginity to one of his mother's maids of honour – a court position for which neither qualities appeared requisite. A little later he fell madly in love with Mary Hamilton, the Duke of Hamilton's twenty-three-year-old great-granddaughter. He wrote to her daily, seventy-five of their letters having survived. 'I not only highly esteem you, but even love you more than words or ideas can express', plighted the

young prince, who with equal banality sent her a lock of his hair.
Mary urged caution, saying that it would be best if they were to
remain just friends. George spurned her advice, until a few months
later he fell for the far more compliant Mary Robinson.

Mary had been born in Bristol, of Irish descent. Her father was
the captain of a whaling ship, who had abandoned his family to
set up a factory run by Eskimos on the Labrador coast. After
marrying Thomas Robinson, an articled clerk, by whom she had
a daughter, Mary was imprisoned for debt, a trauma that, on being
released, left her all the more determined to make her mark and
fortune upon the London stage.

Here it was in December 1779 that the young George first saw
Mary playing Perdita in *The Winter's Tale*. It was a case of princely
puppy love at first sight. During the next few weeks London
gossiped as the heir to the throne wrote daily to his 'Perdita',
sending her locks of his hair and a miniature of himself. He begged
her to come to his apartments disguised as a boy. Mary resisted
his entreaties until, one day returning home from work early, she
discovered her husband in bed with one of their maids. In return
for the immediate satisfaction of revenge, and the promise of
£21,000 when she turned twenty-one, Mary became the prince's
paramour.

It was a nine-day wonder. The two were seen all over town. As
tongues wagged, the king and queen fulminated. Then as suddenly
as it had started George ended their liaison. Scorned Perdita
eventually agreed to hand back his love letters in return for £5,000
down and £500 a year. Thereupon she left for Paris, where she
became the Duke of Orleans' mistress (or so she claimed), before
returning to England to settle down with Colonel Tarleton, the
Member of Parliament for Liverpool. In middle age, paralysed
below the waist, Mary renewed her friendship again with her old
flame. When George died she warmly recalled 'the grace of his
person, the irresistible sweetness of his smile, the tenderness of
his melodious yet manly voice'.[13]

The memory of the Perdita affair evoked a very different
response from the prince's father. Describing it as 'a shameless
scrape', George III (who had to pay for the return of his son's
injudicious correspondence), warned the boy of the dangerous
consequences of 'your love of dissipation'. But the prince spurned
his father's admonitions. His continued drunkenness and dissipation only worsened the breach between the two. The prince ran

Mrs Robinson

18 *The actress Mary Robinson* who as Perdita stole the Prince Regent's heart (Mander and Mitchenson Theatre Collection)

with a wild set that included Colonel Sir Anthony Leger and Charles William Windham. After it was reported that the heir had been riding wildly 'like a madman' in Hyde Park, and had been seen fighting-drunk in both Vauxhall and Ranelagh Gardens, George III had his second son, Frederick, Duke of York, write to warn his elder brother that 'you cannot stand this kind of life'. But he could. As the king had ruefully to admit that practically every day it was 'almost certain that some unpleasant mention of him could be found' in the newspapers.[14]

During his twenties the heir sowed his oats as wildly as he did widely. After a brief fling with Elizabeth Bridget Armistead, a cockney trollop who eventually married Charles James Fox, the politician, he had an affair with Grace Elliott. She later claimed that her daughter, Georgina, was his, even though the child could just as easily have been the offspring of one of her three other concurrent lovers. It was said that the prince begat Lady Melbourne's fourth child (the Prime Minister's half-brother). After liaisons with Augusta Campbell, the Duke of Argyll's daughter, Elizabeth Billington, a pretty singer whose figure ran to chubbiness, and Maria, Countess of Salisbury, an ardent fox hunter twelve years his senior, George fell in love with the Hanoverian envoy's wife.

The prince first met the Countess von Hardenburg in the spring of 1781 at a concert given in his mother's apartments. His first impression of her was of 'a very devilish, agreeable, pleasant little woman'. After their second meeting he thought she was 'divinely pretty'. At the third their eyes met during a card game: the prince was utterly smitten. 'How I love her! How I would sacrifice everything to her!' he declared, 'By Heavens I shall go distracted! My brain shall split!'[15] When she turned him down he quite literally fell ill: when she accepted 'I enjoyed', the prince boasted to his brother, 'the pleasures of Elysium.'

Having learned about the countess's infidelities through the gossip columns of the *Morning Herald*, Karl August von Hardenburg wrote the prince a stinging rebuke, and took his wife back to Hanover. George panicked. He offered to run away with the countess. Then he decided to tell his mother everything. It was an appalling scene: he fainted; she 'cried excessively'; his father did not understand. Perhaps in the hope that guilt might succeed where rebuke had failed the king concluded a long homily on 'your follies', by reminding his heir:

*When you read this carefully over, you will find an affectionate
father trying to save his son from perdition; one who knows
any evil you have acquired is not owing to bad example at
home, who wishes you may become worthy of the situation
that Divine Providence probably intends for you, who knows
you are not wanting in natural talents if you will exert them,
and hopes you have a heart to feel what is owing to those who
have from your tenderest infancy treated you with kindness.*[16]

Even though the prince had to admit that 'The king is excessively
cross and ill-tempered . . . we are not on the best of terms', he did
nothing to placate his parents. Far from it. He made no secret of his
disappointment when George III's recovery from his first attack of
porphyria prevented him from being made regent. At the thanksgiving service held in St Paul's Cathedral in 1789 he and his brothers
behaved abominably, chatting and eating biscuits during the sermon.
The Times raged that the heir was a man 'who at all times would
prefer a girl and a bottle to politics and a sermon'.[17]

By now, to be fair, George had at long last settled down with one
woman. The rub was that she was a commoner, had been widowed
twice, and – worst of all, in an England that was still rabidly Protestant – she was a papist.

Maria Anne Smythe was born in Hampshire in 1756. At the age
of nineteen, after an uneventful childhood, she married Edward Weld
of Lulworth Castle, Dorset. He died a year later. So in 1778 she
married Thomas Fitzherbert of Swynnerton, Staffordshire. After he
passed away in 1781, leaving her a comfortable income of some
£2,000 a year, she moved to Richmond. Here in early 1785 she first
met the Prince of Wales, who was six years her junior. He instantly
fell in love, and to prove the intensity of his feeling stabbed himself
in an apparent suicide attempt. Frightened by his demands that she
become his mistress, Mrs Fitzherbert, a pious Catholic, fled abroad.
George was nigh insane with grief. 'He cried by the hour', wrote
Lord Holland, 'rolling on the floor, striking his forehead, tearing his
hair, falling into hysterics, and swearing that he would abandon the
country, forego the Crown, sell his jewels and plate, and scrape
together a competence to fly with the object of his affections to
America.'[18]

When tantrums failed, and the threat made less than a decade
after the Declaration of Independence, by George III's heir to seek
freedom in the United States did not work, the prince resorted to a

tried and truer ploy. He offered to marry the lady. She accepted, and returned to London, where on 15 December 1785 they were wed in the drawing room of Carlton House, by the Reverend William Butt, an Anglican clergyman who had just been released from a debtor's prison on the payment of £500, and promised a bishopric in the next reign.

Even though in the eyes of the law she was still the prince's mistress, for the 1772 Royal Marriage Act prevented any member of the royal family under twenty-five from making a valid marriage without the sovereign's permission, Mrs Fitzherbert and the Prince of Wales lived contentedly for several years, accepted by their friends as man and wife. They had ten children. At long last it seemed as if George had found someone who could control his malignant ways.

But as the years past, and childbearing thickened Mrs Fitzherbert's figure, the prince's basic malevolence reasserted itself. His drunken bouts became more frequent and more violent. Sometimes he would come home so drunk and angry that Mrs Fitzherbert had to hide under the sofa as George searched for her with a drawn sword. He got so far behind in paying Mrs Fitzherbert's allowance that she had to pawn some jewels to stave off the bailiffs.

Most serious of all, the prince started up with other women. He had an affair with Frances, Countess of Jersey. The daughter of a bishop, wife of an elderly peer, mother of nine children, and George's senior by as many years, she was, a contemporary noted, a 'clever, unprincipled, but beautiful and fascinating'[19] woman, who did all she could to separate her lover from Mrs Fitzherbert by warning him of the dangers of consorting with a Catholic.

The Prince of Wales took no notice of Lady Jersey's advice. After supposedly fathering a child, also called George, by one Lucy Howard, the prince had another liaison with Anna Maria Crouch, an opera singer, who had just scored a triumph in the role of Polly Peachum in John Gay's *The Beggar's Opera*. Her husband, a lieutenant in the Royal Navy accepted £400 a year in return for not suing for the alienation of his wife's affections. Anna Maria did even better: she got a £12,000 bond in return for a comparatively few nights' work.

Not surprisingly, by now the prince's debts were so staggering that he was reluctantly forced to conclude that the only way to repair his finances was to take a lawful wife. In return for an heir the nation would show its gratitude by rewarding the father with a much increased pension.

19 *The wedding of the Prince Regent and Mrs Fitzherbert* in 1785. Anonymous cartoon (Mary Evans Picture Library)

BEGGARS OPERA.

De Wilde del.

Thornthwaite sc.

Mrs CROUCH as POLLY.

London Printed for J. Bell British Library Strand Feb 1.1791.

20 *Anna Maria Crouch* as Polly Peachum in 'The Beggar's Opera' in 1791 (Mander and Mitchenson Theatre Collection)

Once George decided that he must marry, he did not appear to be particularly concerned about the choice of a bride. Indeed, it almost seemed as if he selected Princess Caroline of Brunswick as a perverse protest against having to wed in the first place. Lord Holland thought Caroline to be 'exceedingly loose' even for a German principality 'where at that period they were not very nice about female delicacy'. While Lady Jersey had urged the prince to take a legal wife so as to bring her rival, Mrs Fitzherbert, down to her own level as a mere mistress, she did everything possible to prevent the marriage from working. She insisted, for instance, on being made a Lady of the Bedchamber of the new princess, and delayed the departure of the coaches to Greenwich so that there was no one to officially welcome Caroline when she first landed in England.

But Lady Jersey's machinations were not needed, for the marriage broke down of its own accord, well before it was consummated. At first sight the betrothed couple took an instant and abiding dislike to each other. On being introduced to his bride George appeared to pall. He turned to Lord Malmesbury, the diplomat who had negotiated the marriage treaty, saying, 'I am not well. Pray get me a glass of brandy.' When Malmesbury suggested that a glass of water might be more appropriate, the prince refused with an oath, and stalked out muttering something about going to see his mother. 'My God', exclaimed the astonished Caroline, 'Does he always behave like that? I think he's very fat, and he's nothing as handsome as his portrait.'[20]

Soon afterwards, on 8 April 1795, they were married. On the way to the ceremony George confessed to a friend, 'I shall never love anyone but Fitzherbert.' He arrived late, worse for drink. Malmesbury noted that he resembled a man 'going to an execution', and that through his own wedding service he continually ogled Lady Jersey. Most people believed that the only night George and Caroline spent together was their wedding night, and that only through the liberal resort to Dutch courage could the prince steel himself sufficiently – for the first and last time – to do the manly duty that England expected.

Not surprisingly the two parted, to return to their sluttish ways. But George's liaison with Lady Jersey did not last for long: they separated on the worst of terms, as he called her 'that infernal Jezebel'.

If anything, the prince's legal marriage to Caroline brought him and Mrs Fitzherbert back together. In the will he wrote in 1796 he described her as 'his true and real wife', while adding the vicious postscript: 'to her, who is called the Princess of Wales, I leave one shilling.'

For well over a decade George and Mrs Fitzherbert lived together, as she grew fatter, and he more unfaithful. It was reported that he had a brief affair with Louise Hillisberg, a dancer, and with Anne, the French wife of the Earl of Masserine. By 1805 he had installed another Frenchwoman, Mme de Meyer in a set of apartments in Duke Street, which he frequently visited late at night. The Prince of Wales accepted the paternity of George Seymour Crowe, the son of a Mrs Crowe of Charles Street, to whom he paid £1,000 as an annual allowance and who served in the East Indies as a major. He also admitted responsibility for William Francis by a Miss Davies.

Even though Mrs Fitzherbert managed to survive the prince's peccadillos with younger and presumably more nubile woman, she could not overcome his infatuation for Lady Hertford. Born in 1760, Isabella was a grandmother of much seniority, who long ago had given up any hope of disguising her age. Wrinkles did not discourage the prince, for, as one court gossip noted, 'older dames' seemed 'to be his taste'. Lady Hertford recalled that George 'threw himself on his knees, and clasping me round, kissed my neck before I was aware of what he was doing. I screamed with vexation and fright. He continued sometimes struggling with me, sometimes sobbing and crying.'[21] Soon after this scene, which went on for hours, George dropped Mrs Fitzherbert. He waited until he became Prince Regent in 1811, before he publicly dismissed her with the humiliating rebuke 'Madam, you have no place.'[22]

As the Prince Regent grew older (and more portly) his taste in women became less athletic. In 1820, the year his father at last died and he inherited the throne, a new favourite attracted his attention. Lady Conyngham was an ample, though still handsome, woman in her mid-fifties with five grown-up children, married to a stolid Irish peer. Scandal sheets speculated about the nature of her relationship with the king:

> *Give the devil his due, she's a prime bit of stuff,*
> *And for flesh she's got conscience enough,*
> *He'll never need pillows to keep up his head,*
> *Whilst old Q and himself sleep and snore in one bed.*[23]

Even though George referred to Lady Conyngham as his 'mistress'

21 *Maria Anne, Mrs Fitzherbert*. Engraving by John Condé, 1792 (National Portrait Gallery)

in truth their relationship was probably as restrained as another scandal monger construed:

> *Tis Pleasant at Seasons to see how they sit,*
> *First cracking their nuts, and then cracking their wit:*
> *Then quaffing their claret – then mingling their lips,*
> *Or tickling the fat about each other's hips.*[24]

While there is no doubt that George IV was fond of Lady Conyngham, for he even lost thirty pounds in weight to try to impress her, in truth the king was a lonely ageing man, desperate for friendship. His one and only daughter, Charlotte, had died in childbirth in 1816. He was estranged from his wife, Caroline, from whom he tried in a messy and failed suit to obtain a divorce.

But George IV's public demeanour did nothing to win him his subjects' sympathy. In July 1821, for instance, he behaved abominably during divine service at Westminster Abbey. Whilst the Archbishop of York, Dr Harcourt, was preaching on the sovereign's duty to protect his people 'from the contagion of vice and irreligion', the sovereign himself was seen 'nodding and winking ... sighing and making eyes', at Lady Conyngham.[25] By his death in 1830 George IV had become so unpopular that his obituary in *The Times* concluded that 'There was never an individual less regretted of his fellow creatures', than the late king. Far from shedding tears, Lady Conyngham's immediate reaction at His Majesty's passing was to purloin as many valuable mementoes of their relationship as she could before someone started to inventory the royal estate. If anyone mourned George it was his most faithful mistress, Mrs Fitzherbert, the only person he had ever really loved, and the woman whose miniature he ordered to be hung about his neck and buried with him in his coffin.

In many respects the new king's career followed that of the old, except that William IV, like most of George III's younger sons, had served in the armed forces. Born in 1765, William had been intended for a naval career since childhood. In 1779 his father first packed him off to sea, rated as an able seaman. The story that the king did so after at least two of the queen's maids of honour had seduced William is improbable. The boy was only thirteen at the time, and thus a little old, if anything, to start a naval career, and a little too young, particularly when poor diets delayed the onset of puberty, to begin an amorous one.

The sailor prince soon became a tremendously popular figure. Englishmen proudly believed the story told about the Spanish admiral, Don Juan de Langara, who after being taken prisoner at the Battle of Cape St Vincent was introduced to the royal midshipman in Gibraltar. 'Well does Great Britain merit the empire of the sea', Don Juan supposedly exclaimed, 'when the humblest stations in the navy are filled by princes of the blood.'[26] William returned to London, the hero of the hour. The audience at Drury Lane gave him a standing ovation when he attended the theatre. His elder brothers were equally keen to initiate him into all the sordid pleasures the capital could offer a young sailor home from the sea. But when William fell in love with Julia Forstescue, and even wanted to marry her, his father felt it safest to send him back to active, and presumably less dangerous, duties at sea.

William fought at the siege of Gibraltar, and in the American Revolution (where Washington's agents nearly kidnapped him). On moving to the West Indies he relished all the pleasures the islands could provide. In 1783, however, the king ordered him back to Hanover to complete his education. William spent the next two years on the continent in dissolute boredom. The claim made by Caroline von Linsingen, the daughter of a Hanoverian General, to have married the prince and have had a son by him is most certainly a figment of her fertile imagination, if only because William's romantic activities emphasized quantity at the expense of quality. Most of his time, he wrote to his elder brother, was spent making love to 'Women as poxed as whores', preferring to perform 'with a lady of the town against a wall, or in the middle of the parade ground'.

Recalled to England in 1785, William was made Captain of HMS *Pegasus*, a twenty-eight gun frigate, and sent off to the West Indies where he returned to his debauched ways. On one occasion he and his brother officers went on so violent a bender that they did £700 worth of damage to Mrs Pringle's high-class bordello in Bridgetown, Barbados. Not surprisingly he caught venereal disease twice. 'Oh for England, and the pretty girls of Westminster', William wrote to his brother, 'at least to such as would not pox me everytime I fucked.'[27]

After siring at least one bastard (also called William), the prince went to Quebec, where he had an affair with Mrs Wentworth, the young wife of the colony's Surveyor General, a staid man in his fifties. To try to hush up the scandal the king recalled William to

England in disgrace. 'The damned women cause me more uneasiness than enough', William lamented. But such regrets were not enough to stop him having an affair with Sally Winn, the daughter of a prosperous Plymouth merchant, who used the liaison to help win naval contracts. 'What! What! What!' exclaimed the king when he heard of the affair, 'William playing the fool again; send him off to America.'[28] So back to Canada the prince returned, where the royal martinet divided his time between flogging and fornication. He went to Jamaica, where he made a spirited defence of slavery, if only because that peculiar institution permitted him to indulge both hobbies with the same folk.

When George III again became ill in 1789 William was recalled home, and after being elevated Duke of Clarence, his naval career came to an end. In many ways this was a pity, for William had been a fairly decent, if limited officer. He would have been a reasonable captain, particularly when he had an efficient first lieutenant and firm admiral to save him from excessive punishments. But since his royal pedigree far exceeded his professional abilities, the prince was beached: profoundly frustrated he looked around for something to do with the rest of his life.

First of all William bought Ivy Lodge, a substantial gentleman's residence in Richmond, where he installed Polly Finch, a courtesan of some repute. She soon tired of the arrangement, particularly when William insisted on spending their evenings reading *The Lives of the Admirals* out aloud to her. Quite clearly the prince was looking for a woman in whom patience was a major virtue.

Dorothea Jordan was born in Ireland in 1761, her mother being a Welsh actress, while her father, one Bland, was a stage hand who claimed to have been a sea captain. At the age of twenty she joined the Dublin theatre company managed by Richard Daly, a notorious whoremonger, who promptly seduced her, leaving her with child. She crossed the waters (or at least the Irish Sea) to come to London, where she adopted the stage name of Mrs Jordan. She was an overnight hit in the lead of *The Country Girl* at the Drury, where, true to form, she took up with the theatre manager, Richard Ford, by whom she had three children.

Dorothea was the leading comic actress of her day. 'Mrs Jordan seems to speak with all her soul', effused Leigh Hunt, 'her voice, piquant with melody, delights the ear, with a peculiar and exquisite fullness.' She was 'the child of nature whose voice was a cordial to

22 *Dorothea Jordan* with one of the 10 children she bore to William IV, on stage as Cora in *Pizarro*. By Samuel de Wilde (Mander and Mitchenson Theatre Collection)

the heart', agreed William Hazlitt, 'to hear her laugh was to drink nectar'.

Prince William first saw this thespian paragon in the spring of 1790. She was playing the part of Little Pickle, in *The Spoil'd Child*, a frothy comedy which gave her puckish sense of humour great scope. She was thirty; he was only twenty-six, his naval career having just come to a premature end. The prince was enthralled, and after pursuing her for eleven months was able to report back to his brothers that 'you may safely congratulate me on my success'.[29]

The couple quickly settled down in domestic stability, in which they lived for the next twenty years, producing a total of ten children, most of whom did well in later life. Frederick became a lieutenant general, while George Augustus ended his days as rector of Mapledurham, Oxfordshire. The girls made excellent marriages: Sarah to Lord De l'Isle and Dudley, Elizabeth to the Earl of Errol, and Amelia to Viscount Falkland. William seemed very happy with their ménage, telling a friend, 'Mrs Jordan is a good creature, very domestic and careful with her children.' Since William's civil list allowance was not sufficient to support this large family, he was not too proud to send his mistress out to work between pregnancies.

> *As Jordan's high and mighty squire*
> *Her playhouse profits deigns to skim*
> *Some folk audaciously enquire*
> *If he keeps her or she keeps him.*[30]

Such meanness, on which the satirists eagerly pounced, damaged William's reputation as a gentleman with the public, and as a son with his parents. Queen Charlotte refused to meet his eldest child by Mrs Jordan until George Augustus was eighteen. Not even Mrs Jordan's behaviour after a lunatic shot (and missed) the king during a performance at Drury Lane Theatre won the queen's approval. As William led the gunman away, she led the audience in a heartfelt, and highly apt rendition of 'God Save the King'.

When Mrs Jordan grew stout and her ability to earn enough to keep him in the manner in which he had become accustomed diminished, William dismissed his mistress. On paper, at least, the settlement he gave her in 1811 was not ungenerous. But the sums he actually paid her were so paltry that to escape her creditors Mrs Jordan had to flee England for France, where she died in poverty in 1816, her bed linen being sold off to help pay for the funeral.

Once more the prince's caddish behaviour invited adverse public comment. One balladeer asked:

What! Leave a woman to her tears?
Your faithful friend for twenty years,
One who gave up her youthful charms,
The fond companion of your arms.[31]

William decided that the only way to restore his finances was to marry a wealthy woman. He first made a play for Catherine Tylney-Long, an heiress worth some £40,000 a year, with £300,000 more in the funds. Wisely she refused him. A couple of years later he set his cap at the Duchess of Oldenburg, the widowed sister of Tsar Alexander I of Russia. After he escorted her and the tsar from Holland on a state visit to England, the duchess confided to a friend that the prince was 'awkward, not without wit, but definitely unpleasant'.[32]

Eventually in 1818 William married Princess Adelaide of Saxe-Coburg. She was a sensible woman, the sort whom every man maintains would make an excellent wife for someone else. They had five children, none of whom lived longer than four months. But apart from that she did William well enough, particularly in view of the material she had to work with. Indeed she deserves much of the credit for the success, or at least the absence of glaring failure that characterized his reign from 1830 to 1837.

Many thought George III's second son, Frederick, Duke of York, pleasant though ridiculous. For instance during his command of the ill-fated British expeditionary force to Flanders in 1793–5, he demonstrated a courage matched only by incompetence.

The Grand Old Duke of York,
He had ten thousand men,
He marched them up the top of a hill,
And he marched them down again.

Frederick's marriage to Princess Frederica of Prussia was equally barren. After it became clear that they were incapable of having children, they split. She retreated to the countryside and her innumerable lap-dogs; he returned to marching his men up and down the Horse Guards parade, and to his paramours.

After a series of affairs, which included one with Letitia Smith, a trollop who simultaneously shared her favours with John Rann the notorious highwayman, Frederick settled down in 1804 with Mary Anne Clark. He was forty, recently promoted commander in chief of the British army; she was an attractive thirty, the daughter of a bricklayer from Bowl and Pin Alley, London. Her humble origins notwithstanding, Mrs Clarke was daring, witty, and amusing. Even though the duke allowed her £1,000 a year, and set her up in high style in Gloucester Place, with three carriages, ten horses, and twenty servants (including three cooks), she was still determined to make the best of the going while it was still good. Thus she took large sums in bribes from officers who sought commissions, promotions, or transfers from the commander in chief.

After Frederick ditched her for one Mrs Cary, Mary Anne Clarke took up with a Major Dillon, and Colonel Gwillym Wardle, the Member of Parliament for Salisbury. In early 1809 they accused the duke of taking bribes, and had parliament set up a select committee of judges to investigate the charges. Wearing a most fetching blue silk dress, Mrs Clarke told the committee of her ex-lover's venality. Although others, such as Elizabeth Taylor, a high class madame from Chelsea, supported her allegations, the worst that could be proven against the duke was poor judgement. He was forced to resign his commission. Public opinion was outraged: in Suffolk and Yorkshire mobs burned the duke in effigy to protest 'the immorality of his life'.[33] After his love letters to Mrs Clarke were read out before the select committee he became so widely recognized as a national buffoon that when people tossed coins they no longer called 'heads or tails' but asked instead 'Duke or Darling?'

As a soldier the Duke of York's younger brother, Edward, Duke of Kent, was even more incompetent, for he combined a mean mind with a vicious nature. In 1790, at the age of twenty-three, he was first appointed to command a regiment at Gibraltar. Edward was an enthusiastic colonel, up early every morning to inspect, drill, and flog the troops. After the men mutinied, he was transferred to Canada, where he continued his sadistic ways. When he sentenced one slovenly soldier to 999 lashes (the most the regulations allowed, and about nine hundred more than the strongest human being could survive) the troops mutinied once more. Eventually the government allowed the duke to go home, and in 1803 even sent him back to Gibraltar, this time as Governor. Reverting to petty sadism, Edward issued 300 pages of regulations which controlled every aspect of the garrison's life, including hair-styles for the officers. When he closed the Rock's grog shops during the Christmas season whole regiments mutinied in protest at being prevented from celebrating their Saviour's birth in the traditional fashion. Dozens were flogged, three were hanged, and the duke was recalled, never to be employed by the army again.

At the end of the Napoleonic Wars, when his debts totalled a crushing £200,000, the duke moved to Brussels, where the cost of living was lower, and British writs for debts did not run. Here he and Madame de St Laurent, who had been his faithful mistress ever since he have been sent to Gibraltar a quarter of a century before, lived as an apparently contented middle-aged couple until, early one morning in 1816, he handed her a copy of the latest *Morning Chronicle*. The paper urged him to cast aside his mistress for a wife, in order to father a legitimate heir, and thus earn the gratitude, as well as the increased allowance, that parliament would vote to those members of the royal family who served the nation in its hour of need. With pained dignity Madame de St Laurent left the breakfast table, and the duke's life, while he returned to the courtship of Princess Victoria of Leiningen which he had been pursuing secretly for the past couple of years.

Edward's youngest brother, Augustus Frederick, Duke of Sussex, behaved in an equally ungallant fashion towards the woman he had not only lived with for several years, fathering a son and daughter, but with whom he had even been through two marriage ceremonies. Born in 1773, George III's sixth son was educated mainly in Germany before travelling to Rome, where he met Lady Augusta Murray and her mother whilst they were inspecting St Giacomo's church. She dropped a handkerchief, which the twenty-year-old prince promptly retrieved. He immediately fell in love with Lady Augusta, who some said was six, and others eight years his senior. A few days after their first meeting he promised in writing to marry his 'amiable Goosy'. A few months later they found a renegade Anglican priest, the Reverend William Gunn, who clandestinely wed them – the 1772 Royal Marriage Act notwithstanding.

Soon afterwards Augusta became pregnant, and the couple returned to London, where they were remarried in St George's, Hanover Square. No one had noticed as the vicar read out the banns in the names of Mr Frederick Augustus and Lady Murray. The following month Augusta gave birth to a boy, and the king discovered his son's clandestine wedding. He ordered Frederick abroad, had the Court of Arches declare the marriage null and void, and confiscated Lady Augusta's passport.

She managed to slip out of the country on forged documents, to join the prince in Berlin, where they lived for some years until he dropped her in 1801 in return for a £12,000 pension, and the Dukedom of Sussex. Five years later he successfully sued to prevent Lady Augusta from using the title 'Her Royal Highness', and in 1809 succeeded in taking custody of their two children away from her. But Frederick at least had the decency to wait until after her death in 1830 before remarrying, this time Lady Cecilia, the widow of Sir William Buggin, 'a city knight' sneered a journalist, 'who was, we believe, a grocer'.[34]

In many ways the story of the illicit amours of George III's children runs the risk of becoming a tedious recitation of greed, infidelity, and ingratitude. Occasionally it is relieved by canards so outrageous that they are patently untrue – such as the one that Lord Graves had slit his throat because the king's fourth son, Ernest Duke of Cumberland, was having an affair with his fifty-year-old wife, and mother of their fifteen children. But most of the allegations contained enough dirt to stick. What disturbed the public was not the immorality of the king's sons, but their amorality. Quite simply they were rotten people. 'There was never a man, of behaviour so atrocious as his – a mixture of narrow mindedness, selfishness, trickery, duplicity, with no object but self, his own ease, and the gratification of his own fancies and prejudices', wrote the contemporary diarist, Charles Greville, of the Duke of Cumberland.[35] He could have just as easily have been talking of any one of the damnedest dukes. It was the sum total of their personal failures as human beings, which they revealed in their most intimate relationships, that more than anything else brought the monarchy to so low a state that even ultra-royalists such as the Duke of Bedford were convinced that it could not survive. In 1819 the poet Percy Bysshe Shelley summed up the royal family's nadir:

> *An old, mad, despised and dying King;*
> *Princes, the dregs of their dull race, who flow*
> *Through public scorn – mud from a muddy spring –*
> *Rulers who neither see nor feel nor know,*
> *But leechlike to their fainting country cling*
> *Till they drop, blind in blood, without a blow.*[36]

VIII

'THE KING'S LOOSE BOX'

When Queen Victoria died on 22 January 1901 and Edward VII inherited the throne, all recognized that an era had come to an end, and anticipated the twentieth century with trepidation. At the last moment the coronation, that most reassuring ritual from the past, had to be postponed for seven weeks because of the king's appendicitis. Edward survived the operation, much to everyone's relief, for it was still a dangerous procedure. But by now most of the foreign dignitaries had left. Vast quantities of specially cooked food, that included 2,500 quails, 300 legs of mutton, *consommé de faisan aux quenelles*, sole poached in Chablis, oysters, prawns, and snipe, had to be given to the poor of London's East End. Apparently they did not find such a diet too rich, for by the time the king was well enough to be crowned, 'popular enthusiasm knew no bounds', recalled Wilfred Blunt.

The poet added that 'a mighty roar of continuous cheering echoed from the Palace to Westminster', as the eight cream-coloured horses drew the king and queen in the crystal panelled state coach to the abbey.[1] Inside lords and commons waited, as did the scholars of Westminster School. Frederick Temple, the ailing octogenarian Archbishop of Canterbury was there, wondering if he would survive the four-hour ceremony. And at the king's express command a place had been reserved for Sarah Bernhardt, Mrs Alice Keppel, Lady Kilmorey, Mrs Arthur Paget, Mrs Hartmann, and other ladies whom His Majesty held in particularly high esteem. One wag irreverently dubbed the pew, 'The King's Loose Box'.[2]

It was a witticism that Edward VII, the only monarch to win the Derby (twice), would have savoured. He made no secret of his liking of fast women and fast horses. He carried on his affairs in a kind and discreet way that endeared him to many people, who were starting to react against the stuffy morality of his mother's day. In many ways Edward's reign was a hedonistic apogée wherein the ruling classes enjoyed the riches and power which flowed from Britannia's might. Of course, the king's love-life does not explain his popularity. Rather it was that ability which allowed him to carry on his affairs with such good nature, and with so little rancour, that also made him an effective constitutional monarch who was able to bridge the gap between the old aristocratic England, and an increasingly democratic Britain.

The creation of the constitutional monarchy owed much to the work of Edward VII's parents, Queen Victoria and Prince Albert. Both were determined that the royal family should come to symbolize the domestic virtues of morality, hard work, and respectability that the new middle classes produced by the industrial revolution treasured.

The young Victoria had no time for the excesses of her wicked uncles. When her first Prime Minister, Lord Melbourne, told her that of George III's sons her father, the Duke of Kent, was 'the best of all' she was very relieved – oblivious that the competition for this dubious honour was far from intense. Her husband, the earnestly boring German princeling from Saxe-Coburg, had no such illusions. Albert was terrified that their children would inherit not only the damnable dukes' profligacy, but his own parents' immorality. His mother, Louise, the Duke of Saxe-Gotha-Altenburg's daughter, divorced his father, Ernest, Duke of Saxe-Coburg-Gotha, to marry her lover, Alexander, Count Von Polzig-Baiersdorf. So nefarious was her reputation, that rumour had it that Albert's real father was a Jewish chamberlain.

Terrified of the gene-pool – or rather the gene-swamp – from which he was convinced their children must spring, Albert overreacted, particularly towards his son and heir. Christened Albert Edward, the poor boy endured an intense regime of early rising and long hours of study, followed by prayer and more study, that was relieved only by healthy food and wholesome recreation. Every minute of his waking day was carefully scheduled, so as not to waste a moment. No frivolity, no boon companions were allowed to sully the training of England's next king. Not surprisingly Edward eventually rebelled.

The first protest came when Albert sent his son to Königswinter on the Rhine to improve his German. One evening after too much wine, the fifteen-year-old prince grabbed and tried to kiss a serving wench. When the news reached England statesmen were appalled. William Gladstone called 'this little squalid debauch . . . a paltry affair . . . an unworthy indulgence'.[3] While agreeing with this harsh verdict of their son's behaviour, Victoria and Albert spurned Gladstone's explanation that it was a result of Edward having been 'kept in childhood beyond his time'.[4] Instead they bridled the boy still more, by appointing General Bruce, a dour martinet, as his governor. After Edward was elevated Prince of Wales, Albert announced that he had not in the least given up his efforts to make him not merely a gentleman, but 'the first gentleman in the country'.[5]

Six years later, after Edward had travelled on the continent, had attended Oxford University (where he was securely chaperoned from the other undergraduates), and made a highly successful tour of the United States, his parents eventually agreed to his earnest entreaty to serve in the army. But their son was not to start with a mere corporal's stripe, or even an ensign's pip. Rather he was to be gazetted as a colonel in the guards, and was sent to learn his duties during summer camp at Curraugh, Ireland.

As usual Albert meticulously laid down the prince's regimen. Edward was to learn an officer's duties from subaltern to battalion commander in ten weeks, a progression which in effect meant that he had to qualify for promotion once a fortnight. The fact that few of Her Majesty's regular officers progressed as far in twice as many years did not daunt the Prince Consort. Albert further stipulated that Edward was not to mess with his fellow officers, but to have an establishment of his own. Here, under General Bruce's supervision, he was to give a dinner party for senior officers twice a week, dine as often in the guards' mess, and accept one weekly invitation to those of other regiments. On Sundays and his other night off, he was to 'read and dine quietly in his own rooms'.

Not surprisingly Edward, at best a slow learner, flunked a course that would have defeated the fastest of intellects. At the end of ten weeks his commanding officer had to admit to serious reservations about permitting the Prince of Wales to command a corporal's guard, let alone a subaltern's platoon. Albert had to console himself that his son's lack of progress was typical of 'the idle tendencies of English youth'.[6]

Only in one activity did the heir display both energy and aptitude. Towards the end of the summer camp, after a boisterous regimental guest night, some fellow officers smuggled Nellie Clifden into Edward's bedroom. She was a pretty young actress, one of the stable of easy girls whom rich guardees kept like polo ponies as part of their baggage train. Apparently Edward and Nellie both enjoyed the experience, for he spent much of the rest of his life repeating it as widely and as frequently as possible, while she returned to London to tell all who would listen.

Soon after Edward left the army to start the autumn term at Cambridge, stories of his son's escapade reached Albert's ears. He could have not been more mortified. On 16 November 1861 the Prince Consort wrote to the deflowered lad 'with a heavy heart about a subject which has caused me the greatest pain I have felt in this life'. Reserving for the loss of the boy's virginity the anguish that a Victorian paterfamilias would usually retain for the extra-marital violation of his daughter's hymen, the Prince Consort reprimanded Edward that this fall was 'a piece of gross and deliberate cruelty'. What might happen if Nellie got pregnant? She would blame the prince no matter how many men she had laid with! His name would be dragged through the courts! He must not pay a penny! Unlike Charles II, the Prince Consort was quite willing to let poor Nellie starve.

Deeply distraught, and unable to sleep, nine days later Albert hired a special train to take him from Windsor to Cambridge. By the time he arrived at Madingley Hall, the Jacobean House five miles west of the university where Edward had been lodged to spare him from the city's temptations, Albert was feeling terrible. The chill he had caught three days earlier inspecting the Staff College at Sandhurst in the rain, worsened. The father–son talk they had striding the lanes around Madingley (which was painfully prolonged because Edward got lost) made him sicker, and by the time Albert arrived back at Windsor Castle early the next morning he was weak and aching all over.

The first definite symptoms of typhoid fever appeared on 7 December. The doctors reassured the queen that there was nothing to worry about – advice which prompted one courtier to observe that they were 'not fit to treat a cat'. Unfortunately he was right, and the medical men were wrong. A week later Albert died at the age of forty-two. Queen Victoria was distraught. Encouraged by the opinion of Sir William Jenner, the leading typhoid specialist of the day, that 'great worry and far too hard work' had contributed to the tragedy, she blamed Edward for his father's death. 'I never can or shall look at him without a shudder',[7] she told her eldest daughter. To get rid of him she dispatched him on a tour of the Holy Land.

Cognizant of the Prayer Book's advice that one of the chief benefits of matrimony is the avoidance of fornication, the queen and her counsellors decided that the wisest thing to do was to marry Edward off to some sensible girl as quickly as possible. After surveying the princesses of Europe to find one who was both prudent, Protestant, and presentable, they selected Alexandra, the daughter of Christian IX of Denmark. She was only sixteen, with a cool beautiful face and 'lovely figure, but very thin'. Called Alix by her friends, the princess exuded a sense of gay innocence. Attracted by the prospect of marrying into Europe's leading royal family, and leaving the poverty of her own (where she had to mend old coats rather than buy new ones), she was not as upset as Victoria and Albert had been to learn from her prospective mother-in-law that her fiancé would not approach their wedding night as unsullied as she.

They were married on 10 March 1863 at Windsor Castle. It was a sober ceremony, the mood of which the Poet Laureate, Tennyson, managed to capture in his turgid verse:

> Sea King's daughter from over the sea Alexandra!
> Saxon and Norman and Dane are we
> But all of us Danes in our welcome of thee![8]

The 'Sea King' himself was not present, since Queen Victoria refused to invite any one with so notorious a reputation for promiscuity as Christian IX. Immediately after the ceremony Victoria hustled the happy couple to Albert's tomb, where they were photographed coyly eyeing each other, as the groom's mother intently stared at a white marble bust of her late husband.

Their marriage started well enough, as they tried to find something to do with their time. They set up house, they opened bridges, cut ribbons at town halls, laid foundation stones, were presented keys to cities and scrolls from loyal associations, travelled on the continent, and with an efficiency that had made Great Britain the workshop of the world shot large numbers of God's creatures.

Edward and Alix helped redress the balance of all this killing by bringing six children into the world in just over seven years. But

23 *The wedding of the Prince of Wales*, future Edward VII, to Princess Alexandra in 1865, by Sir William Frith (By gracious permission of Her Majesty The Queen)

after they had fulfilled the heir's first duty of providing more heirs, there was nothing much of meaning left for them to do. Edward quickly tired of the trivial round of royal duties, while Alix found the constant reproductive round a physical burden. The birth of her third child, Louise, in 1867 nearly killed her. She developed rheumatic fever which left her with a permanent limp. Edward's attitude to his wife's suffering was uncharacteristically callous: it took three telegrams, of mounting stridency, to persuade him to return from the Windsor races to see her. He was more understanding during the birth of their last child, John, who died a day later, the delivery having been botched by the local GP who was called in to handle the emergency. This sad episode almost certainly ended the physical side of the Wales's marriage.

Bored and underemployed, Edward sought diversions elsewhere. At first he found them when Alix was off visiting her tedious family in Denmark, or else sought them abroad.

Princess Vicky, Queen Victoria's eldest daughter, who married the Kaiser of Germany, once complained to her mother that 'the French make improper things interesting, and gloss wickedness over'. Edward agreed. That is why he found France and its women so seductive.

During the last few years of the Second Empire both were gloriously exciting. Napoleon III was rebuilding Paris with its magnificent boulevards as a fine city in which artists could flourish, to which composers such as Offenbach could bring a sense of hedonist gaiety, and where the dancers of the newly founded *Folies Bergère* could flaunt an open sexuality. French society was masculine without being macho. In it men (and women too) could indulge every human appetite with style and without guilt. This was a time of gorgeous excesses. Great chefs commanded high salaries for their creations. Fine courtesans, known as *les grandes cocottes*, sold themselves for gigantic sums which all who could afford considered well worth the price. Coral Pearl, for instance, received £10,000 from the Emperor himself for just one night. She once catered to her customers' love of fine food and finer women by having herself served up to a group of gourmets in a silver platter carried in by four waiters, naked except for a sprinkling of parsley.

Edward found the honest sexuality and cheeky humour of French women most alluring. When La Goulue, the uninhibited dancer at the Moulin Rouge shouted out as he entered, 'Ullo Wales! Est-ce que tu vas payer mon champagne?' the Prince happily ordered bubbly all around for the dancers and the band. Edward's favourite *demi-monde* was Hortense Schneider, a singer who after performing in Offenbach's operas would retire to the prince's private dining room. The Marquis of de Villemer called Hortense 'exciting, modern, ironic – the froth of the champagne'. She was a generous woman, a little bit of a snob, whose penchant for sleeping with royalty earned her the title *le passage des princes*.

Hortense was not the only courtesan with such ambitions. When the Duke of Grammont-Caderousse presented Guila Barucci (who used to boast that she was the 'greatest whore in the world') to Edward in his private dining room, she curtsied, and promptly dropped her clothes to the floor. The Duke reprimanded her. 'But you told me to be on my best behaviour with his Royal Highness', she answered, 'I showed him the best I have and it was free.'

A few years later the prince discovered that Guila's worst came rather expensive. Following her death from consumption in 1871, the indiscreet letters that he had sent her were put on the market. It took a long and delicate set of negotiations before her brother was prepared to sell them for £240. Edward failed to heed his friend, Rosa Lewis, the cockney cook, hotelier and whore, who advised 'No letters, no lawyers, and kiss my baby's bottom.'

Until Rosa opened the Cavendish Hotel, upper-class men had problems finding places for their trysts. Edward preferred to seduce their wives at tea time – when the husbands were supposed to be at their club (or else partaking of tea and sympathy with someone else's spouse). Sometimes Edward could not arrange a tea-time tryst, and had to resort to a night-time ride in a Hackney. After one such ride he gave the driver but a shilling, being ignorant of the appropriate fare.

'What's this bleeding bob for?' asked the indignant cabby, who had not recognized his customer.

'Your fare, my man,' he replied.

The prince's companion managed to quiet the cockney's tirades about 'a bleeding bob for two hours driving and ten miles', by giving him two sovereigns.

'I knowed you was a lady as soon as I seen you,' the driver acknowledged, before scornfully asking, 'but where did you pick 'im up?'[9]

Edward characteristically used to tell this story against himself. The remarkable thing about his escapades was how few people they hurt. Upper-class men and women were taught to bear their spouses' infidelities with the self-control of their caste, as they solaced themselves by being just as, if not more promiscuous. Children, of course, had no such consolation particularly when their mothers received lovers at home.

In 1874 Edward visited the Princess de Sagan, an old friend, in her castle at Mellow, south of Paris. Her eldest son entered the boudoir to find a gentleman's clothes spread all over the sofa. Outraged he gathered them up, ran downstairs, and threw the lot into a fountain. When Edward emerged from the bedroom, he had nothing to wear, and had to return to his lodgings wearing an extremely tight pair of borrowed trousers. Neither mother nor lover were understanding, and the offending adolescent was banished from home.

Another remarkable thing about Edward's escapades is how few bastards he produced. Some speculated that he was the real father of the Princess de Sagan's younger son, and there are stories that one of his sprigs lived to a ripe old age in La Jolla, California. Of course, many people claimed royal blood, and some possessed similarities. But considering Edward's proven fecundity with Alix, as well as the uncertain methods of birth control (of which the prince refused to avail himself), it is surprising that he only sired one authenticated bastard.

The details are understandably murky. Lady Susan Pelham-Clinton was the daughter of the fifth duke of Newcastle. Her mother, the Duke of Hamilton's daughter, eloped in 1850 with a Belgian courier, being pursued across the continent by the young Mr Gladstone. Ten years later Susan demonstrated similar impetuousness by insisting on marrying Lord Adolphus Vane, notwithstanding the fact that her father was heartbroken and her friends unanimous in their condemnation. 'Lord Adolphus is a good creature', admitted one of them, 'but between drink and his natural tendency to madness there is a sad prospect for Susan.' After seven years of unhappy marriage Adolphus died insane, leaving a relieved widow.

Immediately afterwards she met the Prince of Wales, who was only too happy to console the bereaved. 'You have shown me so much kindness over the last two years', she wrote to Edward in the autumn of 1871, when she was seven months pregnant with his child, and desperately needed money: 'Without any funds to meet the necessary expenses and to buy the discretion of servants it is impossible to keep this sad secret.'[10] So the prince packed Susan off to Ramsgate, arranged for her to be given £250 for expenses, and sent his personal physician, Dr Oscar Clayton, to attend to 'the event'. Although details about the child's fate and birth are unknown, the confinement much weakened the mother, who died three years later.

Far more public was the prince's involvement with another woman, who too suffered badly from the toils of childbirth. In February 1868, the twenty-year-old wife of Sir Charles Mordaunt gave birth to a premature son. Insane with grief she told her husband that the child was not his. 'I have done very wrong', she hysterically admitted, 'with the Prince of Wales, and others, often and in open day.' Rather than taking this confession as the symptom of a mind deranged by grief (for most Victorians regarded making love in the daylight as a sign of pronounced instability), Sir Charles broke into his wife's desk where among other things he found letters from the Prince of Wales. Even though there was nothing incriminating about them, for Harriet and Edward had been friends since childhood, the prince was subpoenaed to give evidence at the divorce trial.

When hearings opened the following April it was as if monarchy itself was in the dock. On being asked by counsel 'Has there ever been improper familiarity or criminal act between yourself and Lady Mordaunt?' the prince unflinchingly declared, 'There has not.' A muted round of applause greeted this answer. Counsel declined to cross-examine, and Sir Charles lost his case on the grounds of his wife's insanity.[11]

None the less, the whole affair severely damaged the monarchy, particularly when combined with a growing sense of aristocratic dissipation, and Queen Victoria's excessive mourning for Prince Albert.

The Mordaunt case was but one of a series of high society scandals which upset middle-class morality. After the Earl of Wicklow's heir passed away in a brothel, his widow tried to palm off an adopted child as sired by the earl so as to keep the title. Lord Willoughby d'Eresby, the Joint Hereditary Grand Chamberlain of England, fleeced his French mistress of thousands of pounds before eloping with her maid. Lord Euston tried to have his marriage annulled on the grounds that his wife was a bigamist, only to discover that she was in truth married to him, because her first 'husband' was already married. The Marquess of Hastings released 200 rats in a high-class bordello as his friends turned out the lights, and locked the doors. Far from being amused, Queen Victoria warned her son that the excessive behaviour of the aristocracy 'resembles the time before the First French Revolution'.[12]

Indeed the red hat of Liberty was once again seen in the streets of London, where talk of republicanism reached heights unknown since Cromwell's day. 'The present prince should never dishonour his country by becoming its king', wrote Charles Bradlaugh, 'neither his intelligence . . . nor his virtues entitle him to occupy the throne of Great Britain.'[13]

But public opinion turned out to be as fickle as it had been outraged, particularly after Disraeli enticed the queen from mourning, and the Prince of Wales nearly died of typhoid fever in 1871. Following the Mordaunt affair the rabble had hissed Edward and Alix at Ascot: a year later they cheered his latest love as she rode elegantly along Hyde Park's Rotten Row.

Lillie Langtry was born in the island of Jersey, where her father, the Very Reverend William Corbet Le Breton was dean. He was, Lillie recalled 'a damned nuisance' who 'could not be trusted with any woman anywhere'.[14] Her father had to warn her to give up her first boyfriend lest unwittingly they commit incest because he was one of the many wild oats the Very Reverend had sown. Thus by the time she was twenty Lillie was only too eager to leave home.

The opportunity came when she saw the *Red Gauntlet* sail into St Peter Port harbour. This beautiful yacht belonged to Edward Langtry, a bland sporting gentleman, old at twenty-six, recently widowed, and with riches from Belfast shipyards that were beyond Lillie's dreams, although not her ambitions. 'To become the mistress of the yacht, I married the owner', she candidly admitted. Neither turned out to be much of a success. Lillie soon tired of Edward's yachting, and incessant fishing. Edward, who according to Lilly was 'extremely shy', found no passion in their marriage except for an inchoate jealousy. Whenever complimented on Lillie's luminous beauty, her husband would reply, 'Oh, you should have seen my first wife.'[15]

Bored, their indifferent marriage in decline, the Langtrys came to London in 1877, where Lillie was an instant success. Lord Randolph Churchill told his wife, Jennie, that at Lord and Lady Wharncliffe's he 'took into dinner a Mrs Langtry, a most beautiful creature, quite unknown, very poor, and they say she has but one black dress'.[16] The society artist, Frank Miles, asked her to sit for him, and sold thousands of photographs of his drawing. John Everett Millais was widely believed to have portrayed her as Effie Dean in his highly acclaimed narrative painting based on Sir Walter Scott's *The Heart of Midlothian*. Although too sentimental for modern tastes the Victorians loved this picture of an eager maid hurrying to meet her outlaw lover, innocent that he would betray her. The painting was so popular that velvet ropes were used to keep back the crowds at the Royal Academy exhibition. Even more popular was Millais' full-length portrait, which showed 'The Jersey Lily', simply dressed and holding the flower that shares her name.

Mrs Langtry quickly became a celebrity who attracted the enthusiasm of the multitude, and the propositions of the well-heeled. She succumbed to both. Queen Victoria's son, Prince Leopold paid court to her, as did Rudolph, the spoiled Crown Prince of Austria. The competition between her admirers grew so intense that the Earl of Lonsdale and Sir George Chetwynd had a fist-fight in Hyde Park over who should take her out riding, and the Duke of Portland had to separate them – much to the public's amusement. Morton Frewen, an extremely rich young Englishman, gave Lillie his favourite horse, Redskin, in return for her ultimate favours. Afterwards he recalled that 'lilies can be so dreadfully boring when not planted in a bed'.[17] Frewen was a bad loser, for when he realized that he could not compete with the Prince of Wales he went off and became a cowboy in Wyoming. He was not alone in his disgust.

In a rare display of pique – or for that matter of any passion – Edward Langtry held up his wife's blotting paper in the mirror to try to read her correspondence, prompting Lillie to order the servants to change it daily.

The Prince of Wales, as leader of high society, soon became interested in this new creature on the London scene, and made a special trip to see the Effie Dean painting. He first met Lillie in May 1877 by pre-arrangement at the house of Sir Arthur Young, the Arctic explorer. Alix was away staying with her brother in Athens. Within a month Edward and Lillie were seen together everywhere, and she was accepted as the prince's first official mistress.

The attraction was not merely physical, although Lillie did go to the trouble of having her négligés trimmed in ermine to amuse her lover. Lord Suffield, the prince's intimate friend, thought that she captivated Edward because she refused to let him dominate her. They were equals who suited each other emotionally as well as physically. Both lacked sentiment, she never complained, and (unlike Alix) she was always on time.

To be able to enjoy each other in domestic privacy Edward built a villa for Lillie in Bournemouth, which he gave to her through an intermediary, the Mordaunt affair having taught him the need for discretion when rewarding other men's wives. Lillie furnished the

villa to please their tastes, with a large guest suit for the prince, and
adjacent a smaller bedroom for herself. She had a small hatch cut
high in a wall so the prince could inspect the guests before coming
down for dinner. On one wall she painted the challenge 'They say
– What say they? Let them say'. On another she carved 'Dulce
Domum' to mark the illicit excitement and sweet domesticity she
provided the prince.

Such domestic simplicity did not, however, imply domestic fidelity. Edward continued his ways, having a well-publicized liaison
with Sarah Bernhardt, the French actress, who in old age boasted 'I
have been one of the great lovers of my century'.[18] Soon after Sarah's
arrival in London as part of a French touring company she found her
way to the prince's bed. After one visit she sent a note apologizing to
her director, 'I have just come back from the Prince of Wales, it is
twenty past one. I can't rehearse any more at this hour. The Prince
has kept me since eleven.'[19]

As Edward tired of Lillie, he encouraged his mistress to seek her
fortune on the stage, her husband having gone bankrupt. The prince
sent Lillie roses for the opening night at Manchester of the provincial
tour of *She Stoops to Conquer*. Royal patronage helped Lillie become
a great success in England. But she had to make it on her own in
republican America. And she did, becoming a great success on the
other side of the Atlantic. Several American millionaires proposed
to her, many more slept with her, while West of the Pecos Roy
Bean, the Texan judge, tried and hanged horse thieves in the tavern
which he dedicated to the 'the Jersey Lilly'.

As Lillie left off with the prince she took up with Louis
Mountbatten and had a daughter, Jeanne-Marie. The ambitious
young naval officer (who went on to become First Sea Lord, and
the Duke of Edinburgh's great uncle) would have married Lillie had
not she still been yoked to Edward Langtry. Lillie's depression at
being ditched by the father of her illegitimate child, worsened when
she learned that her favourite brother, Maurice, had been killed
trying to shoot a man-eating tiger in India. So she drifted from man
to man. When asked why she put up with George Baird, a sadist
with half a million a year to spend, she replied, 'I detest him, but
every time he does it he gives me a cheque for five hundred pounds.'[20]
Eventually Edward Langtry died, emotionally and financially
broken, freeing Lillie to marry Hugo, Baron de Bathe. But the
match brought her little happiness. Lillie became estranged from her
daughter, and eventually died in Monaco in 1929.

The Prince of Wales's next mistress was just as flowery as the Jersey Lily. Frances Greville, Countess of Warwick (known to her friends as Daisy) was one of the richest and most beautiful women of the age. On the same day that she turned down Prince Leopold's proposal, she accepted one from Frederick, Lord Brooke, the Earl of Warwick's heir. Apparently she preferred to marry someone of uncertain sexual preferences to Queen Victoria's son, a known hae-mophiliac. Anyway both men took it like gentlemen. Like a good sport Brooke asked Leopold to be his best man at the wedding, and afterwards tolerated his wife's many affairs.

Daisy had an extraordinary passionate liaison with Lord Charles Beresford, another ambitious naval officer, and friend of the Prince of Wales. So true was their illicit love that Charles vowed to sleep only with his mistress. Thus when Lady Beresford became pregnant, Daisy felt betrayed and sent her lover an irate note. As bad luck would have it Charles was away on his ship, and had given his wife a *carte blanche* to open all his correspondence. Having read the letter, Lady Beresford showed it to the Prime Minister, who advised her to give it to the custody of George Lewis. He was the high society solicitor, whose discretion was so great, and whose secrets so damaging, that half the leading families in the land gave a collective sigh of relief when his files were burnt on his death.

Realizing her indiscretion, Daisy went to see the Prince of Wales. Always susceptible to a lady in distress – particularly when they made no pretence of being maidens – Edward raised the matter with Lewis. When Charles Beresford heard what had happened, he rushed home from the Mediterranean to have a particularly volatile interview with the prince, whom he almost struck and called a blackguard and a coward. Edward threatened the Beresfords with 'social death': he would never again receive them, or anyone else who invited them to their homes. Charles Beresford retaliated by saying he would tell the gutter press all he knew about the prince's affairs. The fracas hurt Edward's marriage, for Alix refused to return from Denmark for his fiftieth birthday. Eventually an apology was patched up, Beresford returned to sea, Alix learned to lump it, and Daisy entered Edward's bed.

She remained the prince's mistress for about a decade, the most passionate love of his life, whom he called 'my own adored little Daisy wife'.[21] Lady Warwick even had a special railway station built at Eaton Palace, her husband's ancestral seat, so the prince could visit her more conveniently. On such meetings, however, Daisy recalled Edward might be 'bothersome, as he sat on a sofa, holding my hand, and goggling at me'.

It was the prince's wish to be close to Daisy which led to the most damaging scandal of the day, the Tranby Croft Affair. He had hoped to have been able to stay with her at the house of mutual friends in Yorkshire. But a series of accidents meant that he had to pass the week of the Doncaster Races at Sir Arthur Wilson's house in Tranby Croft. At the prince's suggestion the guests gambled at baccarat, a game that was as expensive as it was illegal. When Lieutenant Colonel Sir William Gordon-Cumming, Commanding Officer of the Scots Guards, was caught cheating, his fellow guests forced him to sign a confession, to which the prince was a witness. On second thoughts Gordon-Cumming withdrew his confession and sued for libel. Edward attended all but one day of the trial. Even though Gordon-Cumming lost his case, the prince's involvement in this squalid affair horrified all segments of society. Queen Victoria wrote to her daughter, 'it is a fearful humiliation to see the future king of this country dragged (and for a second time) through the dirt'.[22] Edward's high rolling outraged Non-conformist opinion. A deputation of aristocratic ladies went to beg the Archbishop of Canterbury to warn the heir of the consequences of his wicked ways.

But once more the prince's unpopularity was as shallow as it was intense. The British public greeted the news that his horse, Persimmon, had won the 1896 Derby with the enthusiasm that they normally reserved for a major victory abroad or the end of a world war. Edward's traditional Derby night dinner at Marlborough House for the members of the Jockey Club was a personal triumph, which he capped with a midnight supper, and bed with his current inamorata, Georgina, Countess of Dudley.

During the last years of his mother's reign Edward met Alice Keppel, the mistress with the most political influence. She was the youngest daughter of Admiral Sir William Edmonstone, and had married George Keppel, the Earl of Albermarle's brother, an army officer and gentleman, who accepted his wife's infidelity with the *savoir-faire* expected from his class (and for which Edward VII awarded him the Royal Victorian Order). Edward and Alice met in February 1898, when he was fifty and she twenty-nine. Straightaway they became lovers and remained such until Edward died in 1910.

All agreed that Alice Keppel was a most remarkable woman. She was extremely beautiful, even for one of Edward's mistresses, with a fine figure, and an exquisite face. She had a deep throaty voice,

24 *Edward VII* at a country house party at Chatsworth, seated next to Mrs Keppel, here seen looking towards the artist. Drawing by Frank Craig in *The Graphic* (Mary Evans Picture Library)

and smoked with a panache that before the discovery of carcinogens was considered to be the epitome of female sophistication. Alice was good-natured, wonderfully discreet, and her witty asides would charm the king out of his black moods. Once, whilst playing bridge, a game which Edward liked only in the rare rubbers when he was winning (thus making him a far greater threat as a partner than an opponent), the king lost his temper when Alice miscalled. With a smile she apologized that she 'never could tell a King from a Knave'.[23]

Like Lillie Langtry, Alice not only gave Edward physical delights and sophisticated company, but simple domesticity. He adored her children, whom he would dangle on his knee. Sonia Keppel remembered how as a young girl Edward, whom she was taught to call 'Kingy', would amuse her at tea time, by making sliding pieces of hot buttered toast race down his trousers legs.[24]

Recognizing Alice's ability to control the king's anger, friends usually invited both of them to country-house parties. 'She never flaunted herself or took advantage of her position', Princess Alice recalled, adding that 'Aunt Alix . . . welcomed the arrangement.' Indeed, Alix sensibly realized that Alice not only loved her husband and soothed him in a fashion of which she was no longer capable, but that in doing so she helped make her own life easier, and her husband's reign a success. In addition Alice was such a kind and decent woman that the queen came to regard her not as a rival but as a friend and valued ally.

Thus on 6 May 1910, when Edward VII was dying, Alix called Alice to say goodbye to him. By midnight the king was dead. The queen appeared calm, almost serene. Her turbulent marriage was over. She had survived the challenge of many women more interesting, witty, and attractive, and certainly younger than herself, because 'After all', as Alix said, 'he always loved me the best.'[25]

Edward had been a remarkably successful king, particularly in view of his troubled childhood. His parents had overworked him as a boy, and as an adolescent starved him of affection, relaxation, and approval. As the Nellie Clifden affair suggests, he used liaisons to protest against parental restrictions. Denied the ability to fulfil himself as an adult because his mother remained on the throne for so long, not even letting him glimpse at official documents, Edward's appetites remained distinctly adolescent.

He was a prodigious eater, as evidenced by his nickname 'Tum-Tum', and forty-eight inch waist. He would breakfast on haddock, poached eggs, quarter-inch rashers of bacon, chicken, and woodcock.

Both luncheon and dinner would consist of between ten to fourteen courses. Tea was an elaborate meal with tarts, scones, butter-dripping crumpets, cream cakes, and gooey gateaux. He smoked a dozen large cigars and twenty cigarettes a day. Between meals Edward snacked. At the end of his day he would have a meal of lobster salad, cold chicken, a cutlet, or sandwiches. Often he combined his appetites. He used tea time for the seduction of other men's wives, and frequently noted in his diary 'Midnight supper, Lady Dudley'.[26]

Although Edward could be gruff, peppery, and sarcastic, especially towards the end of his life, when his wife became almost completely deaf, and Alice was not around to soothe his moods, his most enduring characteristic was a *joi de vivre*. He had an abiding interest in all sorts of people which Winston Churchill described as an 'extraordinary kindness'.[27] Edward usually retained the goodwill even of those who suffered as a result of his infidelities. His son and heir, George V, a particularly straight-laced and repressed individual, called him 'my best friend and the best of fathers'.[28] Alix once said that 'if he were a cowboy I would love him just the same'.[29] Daisy Brooke felt the same about him. 'He was a very perfect, gentle lover', she wrote, adding that 'anybody would have been won by him'.[30] Perhaps Edward's greatest achievement was not in loving women – for there have always been many ready to serve the crown in such a fashion – but in leaving them. He left few bitter ex-mistresses or vindictive cuckolds, for Edward was as unpossessive as he was kind. Because he never publicly humiliated any of the women he loved – his wife in particular – he managed to retain their regard long after the flames of passion had grown cold.

Basically Edward liked women as people, not as sex-objects. 'It would be wrong to assume', wrote Margot Asquith (who knew him when she was a young woman, but never as his mistress), 'that the king's only interest in women was to have an "affaire" with them. That he had many "affaires" is indisputable, but there were a great many women in his life from whom all he sought was a diverting companionship.'[31]

All classes instinctively responded to Edward's democratic love for his fellow beings. When the Kaiser sneered that the King of England liked going 'yachting with his grocer', he did not understand that Edward's friendship with self-made philanthropists, such as Sir Thomas Lipton, helped modernize the royal family. By letting the *nouveaux riches* such as American millionaires, Jewish financiers, and theatrical folk into high society he dragged England's aristocratic elite into the twentieth century.

Through his love of France, and its women, the king also helped to shift the royal family's foreign focus away from the German links of the Hanoverians and Saxe-Coburgs. It would, of course, be an exaggeration to suggest that Edward's frequent alliances with the ladies of Paris helped produce the Anglo-French *Entente Cordiale*. But without doubt his Francophilia facilitated the work of the politicians.

Since Edward was a constitutional monarch he had little influence on policies *per se*, and his mistresses had even less. Such Lillie recognized. 'If I had been born in the days of the Stuarts', she used ruefully to say, 'I would have been a Duchess in my own right.'[32] Gladstone tried to use her to influence the prince, and thus the queen, but with no success. Daisy Brooke (who in old age as the Dowager Duchess of Warwick was one of the Labour Party's founding members), managed to make Edward slightly more aware of social conditions. 'The workhouses', the Prince of Wales told the House of Lords during a debate on the Poor Law, 'need to be reformed out of existence.' Alice was the most influential, since her regime coincided with Edward's reign. She smoothed over a couple of diplomatic matters, and acted as an intermediary between the crown and the Liberal government of Sir Herbert Asquith, which was elected in the landslide general election of 1906.

As the crown lost the substance of power, it turned to the trappings of pomp to find a new role. Nowhere has this illusion been more significant than in the projection of royalty through the mass media. The end of the nineteenth century saw the growth of the popular press, those penny papers written, one wit sneered, by office boys for office boys. The development of cheap photographic reproduction in the 1860s permitted the sale of large numbers of pictures of 'professional beauties', of which Lillie Langtry was the most enduring. These were all as attractive – and unattainable – as Hollywood stars. They were the first celebrities, the first pin-ups, to be admired at a distance. This was still a deferential age in which the sex objects were ladies of quality, and the man in the street secretly lusted after the women of his betters. In this fashion Edward's affairs anticipated an important aspect of twentieth-century monarchy – the unreal, ever fantastic soap opera, made real by the media, and unobtainable by reality.

At another level, where such public beauties were all too available,

25 *Lillie Langtry* (Mary Evans Picture Library)

Edward and his mistresses played a different role. They shifted the upper classes away from Victorian morality to Edwardian frivolity. If Lady So-and-So's last child did not much resemble his Lordship, few in society cared, and none had the poor taste to comment. Once a wife had done her duty by providing sufficient heirs, she was entitled to some pleasure. The vital point was not how and with whom she took it, but where and how she found it. 'A Scandal was a romance until it was found out', observed Daisy Brooke. 'Virtue, after all', added Lord Suffield, 'is not so much a question of morals as of environments and circumstances.'[33] And so Edward and his circle developed the country-house weekend, with its elaborate, choreographed games of musical beds. Most of the time things passed off without incident or accident. Admittedly there were embarrassing moments. During one house party Lord Charles Beresford crept along the hall to the wrong room, leapt into bed shouting 'cock-a-doodle-doo' only to find himself between the Bishop of Chester and his wife. He left before breakfast.

In many ways Edward presided over a circle that was as brief, as brilliant, as much fun, and certainly as inconsequential as a country-house weekend. At worst his set was as selfish and as boring as, years later, Daisy Brooke thought. 'I can't remember one friend of mine that was happy.' And at best Edward's affairs spiced up a *fin de siècle* that was to destroy itself in the carnage of the First World War.

IX

'THINGS WERE DONE BETTER IN MY DAY'

At one thirty in the afternoon of December 11th, 1936, at the same time as the Clerk of the House of Commons gave the traditional royal assent, 'Le Roi le veult', to the Act of Abdication by which Edward VIII renounced the throne to marry his mistress, the cream of London's high society was lunching at the Ritz. Alice Keppel was at the hotel. Although looking, someone recalled, 'rather formidable and slightly coarse', Edward VII's erstwhile mistress summed up the abdication crisis with a devastating mot: 'Things were done better in *my* day,' she observed.[1]

Mrs Keppel could have not been more correct. While Edward VIII dealt the crown a blow which has served as a terrible warning to his successors, Edward VII, whose escapades were far more varied, and much healthier, left the monarchy as strong, if not stronger than when he inherited it from his mother. The difference between the two Edwards was not one of morality but rather of style, of kindness, of a sense of duty, and of the realization that the monarchy no longer ruled, but reigned over a constitutional democracy.

Edward VIII's fundamental problem was not that he had a mistress, but that he wanted to turn her into both his wife and the queen of England. Unable to get his way he renounced his patrimony, because, as he told the world on the BBC radio, 'I have found it impossible to carry the heavy burden of responsibility and to discharge my duties as King without the help and support of the woman I love.'[2]

Mrs Wallis Simpson was not, of course, the first woman Edward had loved. During the First World War, while in the army, he met Lady Rosemary Coke, Lord Leicester's daughter-in-law. They were practically neighbours, the Leicester family seat, Holkham Hall, being close to Sandringham House. She was, however, twelve years Edward's senior, and, amused and flattered by his attention, may well have taken his virginity and accommodated his passions with that tact and discretion expected from the wives of the aristocracy. In long passionate letters from France, Edward poured out his frustrations at being forbidden to see action, unlike his younger brother, Bertie (later George VI), who commanded a gun turret at Jutland. On leaves Lady Rosemary would amuse and comfort him.

It was on one such leave that Edward quite literally bumped into his new love. He was walking across Belgrave Square one evening in March 1918 when the air raid sirens sounded, so he took cover in the house of Maud Kerr-Smiley (who was by chance Ernest Simpson's sister). Caught in the same raid, Freda Dudley Ward and her escort, one 'Buster' Dominguez, found refuge in the same house. Here in the basement, as Zeppelins buzzed overhead, bombs fell, and ack-ack guns barked, Edward fell in love with Freda. They danced until three in the morning, and after the 'all-clear' sounded, he took her home.

Before he went to bed Edward used ten exclamation marks to tell his diary that he had just met the most beautiful, the most wonderful, the most fantastic girl in the world. Soon after breakfast he sent Freda a letter asking if he might come to tea, and that he would arrive at five if not warned off. Unfortunately Freda's mother-in-law opened the letter since it was written on Palace stationery and addressed to 'Mrs Dudley Ward'. Sixty years later Freda still giggled at this inauspicious start to their affair: 'He and I had a few days of Boxing-and-Coxing around before it was sorted out.'[3]

Freda Dudley Ward was the daughter of Colonel Charles Birkin, of Nottinghamshire, a lace manufacturer, and Claire Howe from New York. In 1913 she married the Right Honourable William Dudley Ward, a Liberal Member of Parliament and Vice Chamberlain of the Royal Household, who spent far more time in the House of Commons than he did with his young wife and daughters. Friends described him as 'charming but vague'.

He was also remarkably tolerant. Very soon after their first meeting Edward and Freda became lovers, as was the habit in the hot-house days of a First World War furlough. When he went back to France he sent her a stream of 'rather schoolboyish letters', and on his return to England phoned her daily to confirm their usual five o'clock rendezvous.

They were a good-looking couple, well suited for each other, both rather slimly built, sharing a zest for life. He was looking for an older, more mature woman, who gave him a sense of domestic stability. Thus he became an honorary uncle to Freda's two young daughters, Penelope and Angela, whom he would take to St James's Palace for tea. In return Edward left his pet Cairn terriers with Freda whenever he went abroad.

Mrs Dudley Ward was both exceptionally attractive and charming, being able to win the affection of everyone she met, from dukes to dustmen. Even though Lady Cynthia Asquith dismissed her as 'a pretty little fluff', Freda had enough sense to realize the limits of her position. 'I never met the King or Queen. They regarded me as a scarlet woman', she recalled, 'Heavens, it was not as if I were trying to marry him. Or even wanted to. He asked me often enough, ardently too. But just as often I said "No." '4

Edward was not completely faithful. On royal visits to the empire he had casual one-night stands with the wives and daughters of crown servants all too willing to serve the crown. In the middle of the 1920s he had a brief fling with Audrey James, the daughter of an American industrialist and English mother. She enjoyed shocking polite society by having herself announced on entering drawing rooms that she was 'Mahatma Gandhi's mother'. Edward, who had courted her before she married Major Dudley Coates, was more successful afterwards. 'He had seen a lot of her in the hunting field, and presently they were having a merry little caper together – merry but brief', noted a mutual friend, adding that 'If I had to guess what cooled him off was that Audrey was too possessive.'5

Mrs Dudley Ward never made the mistake of trying to control Edward, and thus became almost his *maîtresse en titre* – even to the extent of starting, at his suggestion, the Feathers' Clubs (named after the Prince of Wales's insignia) for the relief of the unemployed.

During the 1920s Freda was the most important influence on the heir, which further exacerbated his poor relations with his parents. Their public appearances, recognized and welcomed by sophisticated society, epitomized the style of that frantic age. Like thousands of 'bright young things' they tried to forget the carnage and waste of the war to end all wars in an endless round of parties and pleasure. This was the jazz age, when emancipated women with bobbed hair and flat chests Charlestoned till dawn. 'There were parties every night', Freda remembered. She and Edward might drop by the Embassy, 'the Buckingham Place of nightclubs', to hear the smooth sounds of Ambrose and his band. Or else they would take in the Kit Kat Club, where Leslie Hutchinson, the West Indian singer, would croon his theme song, 'These Foolish Things'. Cynthia Asquith summed up not just Edward's intentions, but those of his generation, when she noted after seeing him dance in some night club, 'He obviously means to have fun'.[6]

Towards the end of the twenties Freda lost influence to another woman. Thelma Furness was the daughter of a United States Foreign Service Officer, who at sixteen had eloped with a bounder twice her age. They were soon divorced, so she could marry Viscount Furness, the shipping magnate, who was notorious for his vile temper, and his fondness for brandy, and for chasing foxes and women.

Thelma joined Edward on safari in Kenya in 1928. Fondly she recalled those nights around the camp fire in her memoirs:

It is hard to convey the quality of those nights, the stars seemed close enough to touch. And the air was like a caress, silent soft. As the Prince and I would feel enveloped in all this, we would instinctively draw closer as if we were the only two people on Earth. This was our Eden, and we were alone in it. His arms about me were the only reality; his words of love my only bridge to life. Borne along on the mounting tide of his ardor, I felt myself being inexorably swept from the accustomed moorings of caution. Every night I felt more completely possessed by our love.[7]

On their return to England Thelma acted as Edward's hostess for weekend parties at his favourite retreat, Fort Belvedere, about thirty miles outside London. 'The Prince of Wales', Bruce Lockhart noted in his diary in September 1931, 'has been going great guns with Lady Furness.'[8] In fact, as Thelma recalled, 'Our life was quiet, even domestic.'[9] They would spend evenings contentedly in each other's company, both doing *petit point*. Thelma bought Christmas presents for the prince's servants, put up the tree and helped him celebrate the holiday.

But early in 1934 Thelma had to go to New York on family

business. On the ship back to England Aly Khan, a lothario who was as rich as he was successful, pursued her. The news proved to be the last straw. Jealous, Edward dropped Thelma, ironically for the woman whom she once called 'one of my best friends'.[10]

The last and greatest love of Edwards VIII's life accepted neither the bonds of friendship nor the limits traditionally placed upon the office of royal mistress. Born Wallis Warfield in Baltimore in June 1896, her father's death when she was young left her with little more than a family name that carried some weight in the State of Maryland. Her mother, whose patrician Virginian ancestors included members of the colonial House of Burgesses, judges, generals, and a governor, had to open their home to lodgers. As soon as she could, Wallis married Lieutenant Earl Winfield Spencer, an officer in the United States Naval Air Service. Handsome, flamboyant, and depressed because his fondness for the bottle had thwarted his flying career, Earl turned into a jealous sadist, who would tie his wife to a bed before beating her. Within three years they separated.

After a passionate affair with a Latin American diplomat (who refused to countenance being involved in a divorce out of respect for the teaching of his church and dictates of his career – which he ended as Argentinean Ambassador to the United States), Wallis quite literally escaped on a slow boat to China. In Shanghai she enjoyed a 'delightful friendship' with a young Englishman, Robbie. In Beijing she started a lifelong relationship with Herman Rogers, a patrician New Yorker, whose family estate abutted Franklin Roosevelt's Hyde Park.

In 1926 Wallis returned to the United States. She established residency in Warrenton, to use Virginia's liberal divorce laws to rid herself of Winfield Spencer. Here she met Ernest Simpson, a business man born of an American mother and English father, who left Harvard in 1918 to serve in the Grenadier Guards, becoming a British citizen. Although Ernest was a rather stodgy fellow, he was a kind and decent man, who offered Wallis security and respectability. Thus she eventually married him in July 1928.

Ernest's business interests took him to London, where they purchased a flat, 5 Bryanston Court, in a new fashionable block, just north of Marble Arch. The couple were happy enough at first, trying hard to break into English society. Wallis's friendship with Thelma Furness helped, for being a royal mistress carried much social cachet.

Although Edward had previously met Wallis at the San Diego naval base in 1920 when she and Lieutenant Spencer were presented to him with scores of other officers and their ladies, he first remembered doing so at Thelma Furness's house in Melton Mowbray, Leicester, in January 1931. Introduced to Wallis and Ernest, the prince made the usual small talk about the paucity of central heating in English houses.

'I am sorry, sir', she answered with a mocking smile, 'but you have disappointed me.'

'In what way?'

'Every American woman who comes to your country is always asked that same question. I had hoped for something more original from the Prince of Wales.'[11]

Edward found such openness (which he always associated with Americans) most attractive. Wallis wrote to her favourite Aunt Bessie that meeting the prince 'was quite an experience'.[12] None the less their relationship took several years to flower. The Simpsons met Edward on four more occasions during the rest of 1931. The following January they invited him to a small dinner party at their flat. It was a great success, going on to four in the morning, and leading to an invitation to Fort Belvedere a couple of weekends later. Since Wallis's health was poor, and the depression had damaged Ernest's business interests, they did not see Edward again until October, when they resumed frequent meetings. By March of 1934 they were so close that the prince sent Wallis a 'bon voyage' telegram when she was about to sail home to America for a short visit. On her return they reverted to their usual partying. 'We went back to his house where we made whoopee until 4.30 am, so you can judge that the party went well' wrote Wallis to Aunt Bessie in June.[13]

So far the prince had considered the Simpsons part of his set: they were just good friends; he was a solid loyal fellow; she was a refreshingly open gal from the United States. But in 1934 this relationship changed. When Thelma Furness went to New York early in the year, she jokingly asked her friend, 'to look after him for me while I'm away. See that he does not get into any mischief.'[14] Wallis and Edward dined alone once or twice a week. After the prince learned of Thelma's dalliance with Aly Khan, they became close enough for Wallis to join Edward on his summer holiday in the South of France. Aunt Bessie came along as chaperone, since Ernest was away on business.

In September, however, Aunt Bessie departed to see the sights of Italy, and the prince chartered Lord Moyne's yacht, the *Rosaura*, to explore the Spanish coast. Wallis recalled in her autobiography that as the *Rosaura* was anchored off Majorca 'we crossed the line that marks the indefinable boundary between friendship and love'.[15] On their return to Cannes, Edward bought her a diamond and emerald bangle, the first substantial gift he had ever given Wallis.

She was blissfully happy. In a note book she kept on the *Rosaura* she recorded her feelings:

Now that we two have met, would that we might drift forever into the dreams that we dreamed tonight.

Without a woman's love no man is safe.

If people had no past, they would have no future.

The man who makes a good lover is the man who loves women first and a woman afterwards.

When Aunt Bessie, back from Italy, warned Wallis of the dangers of her behaviour, she blithely replied, 'You don't have to worry about me – I know what I am doing.'[16]

The problem was that Edward did not know what he was doing, for with precipitous speed he decided that more than anything else in his life he wanted to marry Ernest Simpson's wife. The 1936 New Year's wish he sent Wallis was to 'make us one this year'. The death of his father, George V, and his accession on 23 January left Edward all the more determined to turn his mistress into his wife. Wallis was not so sure. Early the next month she wrote to the new king hoping that 'perhaps both of us would cease to want what is hardest to have and will be content with the simple way'.[17]

A month later, in the first week in March, Edward and Ernest met like two civilized English gentlemen, to discuss the matter in the Simpson's flat: Wallis was away shopping in Paris. Ernest offered to give up his wife if the king promised to look after her. 'Do you really think that I could be crowned without Wallis at my side?' he replied. The following month Edward settled a substantial sum on Wallis, who consulted Theodore Goddard, one of London's leading divorce lawyers. In July Ernest went through the legally required charade of being discovered in bed with one 'Buttercup Kennedy' at the Hotel de Paris, Bray, Buckinghamshire.

Edward and Wallis spent most of August and early September similarly engaged as they cruised the Eastern Mediterranean aboard the luxury chartered yacht, the *Nahlin*. The royal party boarded at Venice, and, escorted by two Royal Navy destroyers, sailed down the Adriatic, stopping at small villages, where they dined *al fresco*, serenaded by the locals. At Sibenik 20,000 peasants in traditional costume welcomed them. At Kotor the cliff seemed to take fire, as thousands of torchbearers greeted the lovers as they watched after dinner from the *Nahlin*'s deck. A few days later as the *Nahlin* steamed through the Corinth Canal the King of Great Britain and Emperor of India could be seen dressed only in a pair of rumpled shorts, standing next to his lady-love.

For Edward and Wallis the voyage of the *Nahlin* was a glorious idyll – the honeymoon before the marriage that the king craved more and more every day. But for the monarchy it was a disaster. Edward flaunted his affair without restraint. Although the foreign papers published details, the British press remained more circumspect. They did not mention Mrs Simpson, air-blowing her out of photographs of the king.

News of the escapade filtered slowly back to England. In the autumn the king was hissed, and several people refused to stand for the National Anthem. The divorce hearings, held in a Lowestoft court thronged with reporters in October, further excited public interest, while freeing Wallis to marry whoever would have her.

Thus on 13 November Major Alexander Hardinge, the king's private secretary, brought matters to a head. He had been a close friend of George V's, and represented the solid – even stolid – virtues of the previous reign. 'Chips' Channon, the diarist, thought him a 'dreary narrow minded fogey'.[18] Edward's reaction to Hardinge's warnings that the English press would not remain silent for much longer, that when the story broke 'the effect will be calamitous', and that he must send Mrs Simpson abroad 'without further delay' was expected. The king raged that 'they had clearly misjudged their man', he would not cave in, this was a deadly insult, and that now, more than ever before, he must marry his mistress.[19]

The denouement came with brutal speed. Three days later the Prime Minister, Stanley Baldwin, advised the king that the British public would not accept a twice-divorced queen. Edward replied that if necessary he was 'prepared to go'. For the next ten days Edward and Wallis pursued the chimera of a morganatic marriage, by which they would be husband and wife but she would not enjoy his rank. Both the Cabinet and the Dominion prime ministers rejected this subterfuge. 'Every thing is wrong and going more wrong', Wallis told a friend when she heard their last hope had been turned down. So on 2 December Baldwin gave the king an ultimatum that he must either forsake Mrs Simpson or abdicate, or else the government would resign. The next day Edward promised Wallis as she was leaving for France, 'I shall never give you up', the news broke in the British press, and that evening the king told the Prime Minister that he had decided to renounce the throne.[20] A week later he signed the Instrument of Abdication, and left England just before dawn on the 12th, to marry his mistress and live with her in futile, bitter exile.

Why?

Explanations for the abdication, which was the essence of Edward VIII's brief reign, and which some have called 'the love story of the century', and others a squalidly selfish action which nearly destroyed the British monarchy, are legion. But obviously they lie in the king's character, and his attitudes towards women, which, like those of most human beings, were shaped during his childhood.

Indeed it could be argued that Edward's problems predated his birth on 23 June 1894. Three years earlier Queen Victoria had selected Princess Mary of Teck as the bride for her eldest grandson, Prince Eddy, Duke of Clarence. The following May the dissolute duke died, leaving his sober younger brother, Prince George, next in line of succession and thus in dire need of a wife. Victoria considered several candidates before she concluded that Eddy's late fiancée was the most suitable. Mary and George were married on 6 July 1893. They had much in common. Both were painfully shy and undemonstrative, with an unyielding sense of duty. For a couple with little expectation of happiness, or capacity for it, theirs was a surprisingly successful marriage. But as parents both were crashing failures.

They failed, for instance, to give Edward much of an education. Looking back over those 'curiously ineffectual five years' under the care of his chief tutor, Henry Hansell, Edward concluded that, 'I am appalled to discover how very little I learned. I am today unable to recall anything brilliant or original that he ever said.'[21] It was probably the precise lack of such qualities, which Edward's father neither possessed nor regarded with anything but the deepest suspicion, that first attracted Prince George to Hansell. A bachelor, educated at Malvern College and Magdalen College Oxford, Hansell was chosen as royal tutor more for his abilities as a golfer and yachtsman than as a teacher. Painfully aware of his short comings, Hansell urged the prince to send his sons to a good preparatory

26 *The Duke of Windsor* at his wedding to Wallis Simpson, six months after his abdication (Radio Times Hulton Picture Library)

school, rather than force them to attend the cramped room in Sandringham House, which had been fitted up with blackboard, desks, and texts, almost to parody the real thing. Only after Prince George found to his horror that Edward could not add up the weight of stags entered in the game book after a day's slaughter, did he hire a tutor to teach the lad mathematics.

'I had a wretched childhood', Edward recollected, 'of course there were periods of happiness, but I chiefly remember it for the miserableness that I had to keep to myself.'[22] The only instructor he thought of with any warmth was Walter Jones, the Sandringham village schoolmaster. This born teacher communicated his love of nature to Edward whenever he filled in for Hansell. During his childhood Edward was lonely, but never alone. He was constantly surrounded by his brothers and sister, cousins, nannies and servants, yet had no real friends. The soccer games that Walter Jones organized with the village schoolboys turned into painful episodes of bruised shins and bruised egos. There was no one with whom Edward could share the rough and tumble, the joy and pain of boyhood. Instead, as he admitted, 'Growing up for me was a prolonged misery.'

His father's decision to send him to the Royal Naval College at Osborne in 1907 only made things worse. The Naval College, housed in Queen Victoria's former residence on the Isle of Wight, combined the philistinism of an English public school with the Royal Navy's traditional brutality. Flogging – albeit without the cat-o'-nine-tails – was rampant. Bullying was encouraged. In his first term the thirteen-year-old prince had red ink poured over his hair and had his neck jammed in a window as a painful reminder to one of Charles I's descendents of what the English people did to kings who displeased them.

After two years at Osborne, Edward was able to move up to the Royal Naval College at Dartmouth, from which he was sent on a three-month graduation cruise aboard HMS *Hindustani*. Even though Edward recalled 'I enjoyed the experience immensely', as a midshipman he did not shine. The *Hindustani*'s captain told his old shipmate, Prince George, 'I would never recommend anyone sailing a ship under his command.'[23]

Even though George V had confidently boasted that the Royal Navy would teach Edward 'all he needs to know', and as King Edward VIII he was an Admiral of the Fleet, the senior service did him no good. While Osborne and Dartmouth might have taught his class-mates the self-discipline, the self-confidence, and a stern sense of duty that enabled them to lead convoys to Murmansk, sink the *Bismarck*, or beat off kamikazes, naval training so scarred the prince that he could only compensate for his hurt by being resolute to the point of self-destruction – in other words by abdicating to marry the mistress who was the antithesis of every value for which the Royal Navy stood. One wit realized this point, when during the crisis of the abdication he observed cruelly how strange it was that an Admiral of the Fleet would prefer to serve a third mate on a Baltimore tramp.

After the Navy George sent his son to Oxford, in spite of his protests that he would not learn anything there. The king selected Magdalen, partly because it was Hansell's old college, and because its president, Sir William Warren, was a tremendous snob, who selected his junior common room for its pedigree rather than any academic promise or performance. Painfully shy, and poorly prepared, Edward made little mark at Oxford. He was a mediocre student, whose intellectual growth was thwarted by being tutored by some of the best minds – and most intimidating personalities – the university had to offer. Few thought much of him as a college man. He irritated his fellow undergraduates by practising on the bagpipes in his rooms late at night. He played golf and tennis, enjoyed hunting and beagling, represented his college in its second soccer eleven, and joined the Officer Cadet Corps (where he eventually reached the rank of corporal). In all, Edward found Oxford a dreadful bore. He left the university without a degree, and with no apparent regrets on either side. 'Bookish he will never be', was Sir Herbert Warren's charitable verdict.[24]

Edward wanted to be a soldier, particularly after the outbreak of the First World War. At the time he was an officer in the First Battalion of the Grenadier Guards, and was bitterly disappointed when his unit was posted to the Western Front without him. 'It was a terrible blow to my pride, the worst in my life.'[25] Even though he begged Lord Kitchener for permission to join his battalion in the trenches, the Secretary of State refused. It was too dangerous to risk the heir to the throne. He might be killed. Worse still he might be taken prisoner.

So Edward had to settle for a staff officer's appointment behind the lines. He inspected the troops, raising their morale, trying whenever he could to share their dangers. On one occasion shrapnel killed his driver. The men always said that whenever the shelling was fiercest, the Prince of Wales would appear. Disdaining a staff car, which would splash mud on tired infantry who stood in the ditches to let it pass, Edward rode miles on a standard army-issue bike, always ready with a smile and wave. In sum, the war convinced Edward that he understood his generation, and they lionized him as one of their own.

Thus like thousands of young men who had seen the horrors of the trenches, Edward held the older generation, whom he blamed for the war, in utter contempt. He wanted to bid goodbye to all that. He wanted to be rid of his father's values, such as duty, self-discipline, respect for tradition, even the crown itself, and to sweep aside his father's prejudices, be they against flying, unpunctuality, turned-up trousers, Americans, or even marrying twice-divorced women. Before he came to the throne Edward had threatened to punish his father by chucking it all in. 'I'm fed up. I've taken all I can stand', he railed to Freda Dudley Ward, after a particularly bruising episode with George V, 'I want no more of this princing! I want to be an ordinary person. I must have a life of my own.'[26] George V recognized this self-destructive streak in his son, confiding to Baldwin that 'After I am dead that boy will ruin himself in twelve months.'[27]

The advent of peace in 1918 confirmed the popularity that Edward first found during the war. For a dozen years he toured the world, being welcomed everywhere with that hysteria which today is normally reserved for matinee idols or pop singers. These tours – to Canada, the United States, Australia, New Zealand, Africa, and Latin America – were a great success, doing much to enhance British prestige, sell British goods, and strengthen the bonds of the British Empire. 'Tell Daddy that we are all happy under British rule' read one sign put up, presumably by the natives, when Edward visited Aden in 1921.

The Prince of Wales found the adulation both attractive and tiresome. While he enjoyed casual copulation with high-born 'groupies', accepting it as droit de seigneur, due the heir on his visit to the more remote parts of the Empire, he found official duties increasingly irksome. Edward got bored, he grew petulant, he was unpunctual. 'What a rot and a waste of time, money and energy, all these state visits are!!' he confided to his diary.[28] In other words, long before he became monarch, Edward was willing to enjoy the privileges of office without fulfilling its equally high duties. Noel Coward noticed that he had 'the charm of the world, with nothing to back it up'. Alistair Cooke was even less generous. 'The most damming epitaph you can compose about Edward – as a Prince, as a King, as a man', he wrote, is that 'he was at his best when the going was good'.[29]

Of course being adored by millions and hedged in by minions would have tried the strongest of characters. Unfortunately due to his parents, Edward's was fatally flawed.

Admittedly George V tried to do his best for his eldest son. 'Now you are leaving home', he told the boy on the train taking them to Osborne, 'and going out in the world, always remember that I am your best friend.'[30] In fact his father was – apart from himself – Edward's worst enemy. A painfully reserved man, King George had to admit that '. . . while I am devoted to children, and good with them, but when they grow up you can only watch them go their own way, and can do nothing to stop them'.[31] Such was perfectly understandable, for George V was a martinet who bullied his children with the lack of mercy typical of those who believe that they are acting from the highest motives. His second son, later George VI, stuttered, perhaps as a result of his father's attempts to break him from being left-handed. Edward was constantly nervous, always adjusting his tie or straightening his cuffs. Both sons smoked incessantly. 'It calms me', Edward explained. It also killed him, for the Duke of Windsor and George VI both died of cancer.[32]

Most of the time Edward tried to hide his feelings towards George V, venting them but obliquely. His father had refused to let him learn to play golf because he was sure that 'If we let those boys on the fairways they would only hack it up'. As an adult Edward became a keen golfer, who characteristically blamed his father for his swing. Much of his second book of memoirs was a diatribe against the way his father dressed. Edward's very first command on becoming monarch was that the clocks in Sandringham House be put back half an hour to Greenwich Mean Time, his father and grandfather having both set them ahead to make the best use of daylight. Unlike his father, whom he recalled had 'an almost fanatical sense of punctuality', Edward was notoriously tardy.[33] Unlike George, who disliked Americans, and was proud of the fact that he had never set foot in that informal and novel country, Edward was so fond of that land, its ways and people, that all but the first of his long-term mistresses had at least one American parent.

Only rarely did the Prince of Wales reveal his true feelings toward his father. He recalled that 'it was once said of him that his naval training had caused him to look upon his own children much as he regarded noisy midshipmen when he was captain of a British cruiser

– as young nuisances in constant need of correction.'[34] Edward admitted that 'It was not easy to please my father.'[35] Only towards intimates would he confess in an unguarded moment, 'My father does not like me', adding after a few more drinks, 'I'm not sure that I particularly like him.'

The ancestor with whom Edward most closely identified was his grandfather. As a young boy he would escape the crowded nursery at York House to walk over to see Edward VII and Alexandra in Sandringham. It was, he recalled, 'a place of perpetual sunlight'. His grandparents spoiled him, letting him stay up late, playing games with him, and giving him glimpses of a raffish world that included Mrs Keppel. 'My grandfather began', he wrote, 'from his earliest youth, to do the wrong thing in the critical eyes of his father, and mother.' Thus becoming king he took the highly significant step of adopting the title Edward, instead of David, the name his parents and family used.

There was however a profound difference between the two Edwards – particularly in their appetites. While the Seventh ate with a healthy gusto, relishing quality as much as quantity, the Eighth was a picky eater who preferred a light lunch of fruit. Their tastes in women were much the same. The Seventh enjoyed them, and treated them decently. The Eighth allowed them to dominate him, or else behaved like a cad. For instance, he let Mrs Dudley Ward know of her dismissal after sixteen years by instructing the royal telephone operator to no longer connect her calls.

Edward's relationship with his mother, more than anyone else, helped shape his feelings towards other women. On the surface he remained very fond of her, never criticizing her in the two volumes of his memoirs. As a man, during his world travels, he carried her photograph in a silver frame to set beside his bed. On the other hand Mary was a poor mother. She found childbirth 'a complete violation to one's feelings', and never understood her first-born. 'What a curious child he is', she once observed. Her shyness erected an unbridgeable gap between the two. 'We talked a lot of nothing very intimate', was how Edward once summed up a meeting with his mother.[36]

Of course, a century ago when servants were cheap and plentiful, upper-class mothers were rarely close to their children. But far from enjoying a warm nurturing substitute nanny, who would protect him from the outside world, and shield him from his aloof parents, Edward's first nanny was a possessive sadist. She would twist his arms and pinch him to make him burst into tears on being presented to his mother and father in the drawing room every night just before bed, so they would hastily hand back the bawling infant to her malignant care. When Edward was three his nanny, whom his parents had never given a day off, had a nervous breakdown, and was dismissed from the royal service.

If Edward rejected his father and his father's values by abdicating, he expressed his ambivalence towards his mother by surrendering utterly to other women. He also liked powerful figures, flirting, for instance, with Hitler and the Nazis until well into the Second World War. (The Führer, who was pretty good at using such men, recognized his flaw, when he observed that Mrs Simpson 'would have made a good queen'.) Others too noticed the same trait. 'The king is insane about Wallis, insane', recorded 'Chips' Channon, 'He, too, is going the dictator way.' Edward's youngest and favourite brother, Prince George, agreed that he was 'besotted with infatuation'. His best friend, Major 'Fruity' Metcalfe, wrote, 'it's very pathetic. Never have I seen a man more madly in love.'[37]

Only rarely did those women he neurotically wanted as both mother and mistress talk about the nature of Edward's love. 'I could have dominated him if I had wanted to. I could have done anything with him!' Freda Dudley Ward recalled, 'He made himself the slave of whomever he loved, and became totally dependent on her. It was his nature: he was like a masochist. He liked being humbled, degraded. He begged for it!'[38]

During his married life with Wallis Edward often behaved like a little boy desperate to please his mother. He would go shopping with her, carrying her packages home. He insisted that the Duchess receive every honour due the wife of an English king, and was bitterly hurt when George VI denied her the title of Royal Highness. He was always doing little things for her: fetching books, getting her sunglasses, rearranging the furniture, lighting her cigarettes, letting her buy whatever she wanted or live wherever she fancied. Sometimes it seemed as if pleasing his wife was the only thing that filled the emptiness of the ex-king's exile. Eventually even she tired of his cloying attention. During the 1950s Wallis had a very public affair with Jimmie Donahue, a bisexual New York playboy, and heir to the Woolworth fortune. They were seen dancing and dining together, blissfully aware only of each other, as the duke glumly looked on. After one especially fragrant episode, Edward was heard to say, 'Darling are you going to send me to bed in tears again tonight?'[39]

It was the plaintive cry of the battered three-year-old to his implacable yet perversely loving nurse, who like a mistress spoiled him, and then reduced him to tears so as to deny him a mother's caress. Most men would have rejected such a mistress/mother. Edward gave up his throne for what Alistair Cooke has described as 'both an adoring lover and a kindly, understanding mother'.[40] And yet Edward never appeared to regret the sacrifice, which he made as much, if not more, to punish himself (and his father), as to please himself by making his mistress his wife. 'I have found her to be utterly without fault, the perfect woman', he told a friend as he lay dying in 1972, 'The Duchess gave me everything that I lacked from my family.'[41]

X
'CURTSY FIRST, AND THEN LEAP INTO BED'

'A royal mistress', Alice Keppel is supposed to have remarked, 'should curtsy first, and then leap into bed.'[1] Once again Mrs Keppel recognized the dilemma involved in princely affairs. At one level the relationship may be part of the normal pleasure of human sexuality. But at another it can become a very serious problem if not handled with tact and restraint.

Stories about the goings on of today's royals are exaggerated and distorted, made even murkier by the glare of incessant press attention. Keeping absolute confidence is the essential condition for proximity to the royal family. If a date talks she is dropped; if friends leak they are discarded; if servants blab they are dismissed, demoted, or transferred to the nether regions of the most distant palace.

Within a contradictory world of aristocratic discretion and media excesses, the British royal family has flourished. Unlike most of the other dynasties which ruled Europe before the First World War, the House of Windsor still occupies the throne. Prince Charles does not need a second class honours degree in history from Cambridge University to tell him that the twentieth century has been unkind to royalty. During the reign of his grandfather, George V (1910–36) five emperors, eight kings and eighteen minor dynasties lost power.

For a brief while it seemed that George V's son, Edward VIII, could have sent the House of Windsor to join all those other imperial dynasties in exile in some seedy sunny watering hole on the Riviera. In ten days in December 1936 Edward VIII went from being the most popular man in the British Empire to a pariah. 'I do not think you ever realised the shock which the attitude you took up caused your whole family and the whole nation', his mother, Queen Mary, admonished.[2]

The abdication was not just a terrible shock to the royal family, but an awful warning about the fickleness of public adulation. The House of Windsor learned this lesson extraordinarily well. Monarchy is a medieval anachronism, chosen by the chance of birth, and endowed with unrivalled prerogatives. Yet in a twentieth-century democracy that – in theory at least – values ability over birth, and individual rights above hereditary privileges, it has gone from strength to strength. As Britain has declined as a world power, and as one or other of its once proud institutions have become financially or morally bankrupt, the royal family has prospered. It has been able to adjust to change with a flexibility that enables it to play a vital role in the life of the nation.

Of course, at one level the House of Windsor has become the 'Royal Soap opera', which Malcolm Muggeridge criticized as 'a sort of substitute or ersatz religion'.[3] But does it matter if millions of ordinary folk escape from their daily round into the rich and famous life-style of England's West Enders? And if a few of the less important members of the cast go off the rails, then the viewers can enjoy the spice; it makes the tinsel all the more credible since most of us can think of relatives who are not without blemish.

On another more serious level the royal family provides several important services. The sovereign is, quite simply, sovereign. She denies politicians the trappings of power. Unlike an American president, who can wrap the most partisan programmes around the great seal of his national office, an English prime minister is put in his or her place. As she peers around a church column during a royal wedding she, like the millions who see her on television, are reminded that the queen, not the leader of the party with the most seats in the House of Commons, is the embodiment of a national loyalty which transcends not just governments but reigns. Prime ministers come and go. The monarch is there for decades, a symbol of national unity. If the sovereign has an heir, and the heir too has an heir, the people can hope that in this uncertain world there will always be an England.

The modern royal family has remained remarkably popular. Since the Second World War the proportion of the British public wishing to see the establishment of a republic has remained at about 10 per cent. The monarchy has been able to revive its popularity through the skilful use of the media. Televised spectaculars, such as royal weddings, or jubilees, have been particularly effective. For instance, after the investiture of the Prince of Wales, an event consciously staged for television, the proportion of the Welsh people who wanted a republic fell to 4 per cent, and the Free Welsh Army became so demoralized that they sold their weapons to the IRA.

Apart from bringing glamour and excitement into ordinary peoples' lives – as well as millions from tourists into their subjects' pockets – the royal family has one other function. It sets standards of personal behaviour, which become all the more precious as they seem to become rarer. At times it seems as if the great British public want it both ways. They like having a religious royal family, yet few of them attend church. On their way to the mammary delights of page three millions of tabloid readers pause for the latest speculation about the royal family. Sometimes it seems as if the modern royal family is a salve for the guilt people feel about the erosion of their own families' stability. It is no accident that the emergence of the Queen Mother as the nation's beloved grandmother figure has coincided with the dumping of the elderly in nursing homes. The public hanker after a stable, harmonious royal family, with all the Victorian trappings of morality, as they find their way into other people's beds and the divorce courts in ever-increasing numbers.

This double standard, these confused and contradictory demands, present the royal family with tremendous problems in the organization of their own lives.

George VI's personality contrasted dramatically with that of his failed elder brother. Restrained, with a stutter that exacerbated his shyness, the new king had a strong sense of duty, a sensible wife, and two nice young daughters. He was a safe family man, who reigned during the dislocation of the Second World War, a time which was far from safe for families. Not a whiff of scandal surrounded the king, neither has it about his equally dependable daughter, Elizabeth II.

The same cannot be said, however, about her sister or second son.

'Princess Margaret was the King's joy', recalled Group Captain Peter Townsend, 'She amused . . . delighted . . . enchanted him.'[4] George VI used to spoil his vivacious youngest child. But when she fell in love with Peter Townsend, an equerry and distinguished Royal Air Force pilot, the royal family objected because he had been divorced. After much pressure the couple called off their plans. Still nursing the hurt Princess Margaret married Anthony Armstrong Jones, a society photographer, in 1960. Their marriage, like so many in Britain in the seventies, broke down. In February 1976 the *Daily Express*, whose new editor was waging a circulation war with its rival flag-waving tabloid, the *Daily Mirror*, published a photograph of the princess and her friend, Roddy Llewellyn, a gardener eighteen years her junior, in the sun-drenched Caribbean Island of Mustique. The fact that the photograph had been cut to exclude the other members of the party, giving the impression that the two were mooning at one another over their rum-daiquiri, did nothing to restrain the gentlemen of the fourth estate. Stories about Roddy and Margaret's visits to a 'hippie' commune in Wiltshire, filled the popular press. The *Sun* pictured one member, 'Sarah Ponsonby, the convent educated niece of the Earl of Bessborough' wearing a pair of jeans, and nothing else, while reassuring its presumably shocked readers that Her Royal Highness had never visited the commune similarly attired.[5]

Tabloid buyers were not convinced. 'Readers Vote NO for Margaret', screamed the *Daily Mirror*'s headlines. Willie Hamilton, the anti-royalist member of parliament, cannily proposed diverting £30,000 from the princess's £50,000 civil list to build a lift for a children's hospital. Recognizing the seriousness of the crisis the royal family closed rank, and portrayed themselves as caring, sympathetic folk, who, like any other decent family were deeply concerned for one of its members in trouble.

The public's reactions to the peccadillos of the queen's second son were very different. While married middle-aged women are supposed to behave with decorum, even nice girls like sailors, particularly those who have helped to win a war. For several years Prince Andrew had been known as 'Randy Andy' because of his enthusiasm for the permissive society – which his father condemned as having 'the moral and behavioural standards of a colony of monkeys'.[6] Presumably Andrew's distinguished service as a Naval helicopter pilot during the Falklands War was enough to mute Prince Philip's strictures. Certainly few condemned him when, as a returned war hero, he had a highly public affair with Koo Stark, an actress. Many were amused, others were envious, and some asked whether the taxpayers should spend £20,000 a year for a prince to gambol in Mustique with Koo, particularly after pictures of her appeared in the tabloids deshabillé, and flanked by the ubiquitous Scotland Yard detective, who clearly gave the impression that a policeman's lot was indeed a happy one. Such fears about the queen's second son were quieted in 1986 when the prince married Miss Sarah Ferguson, a career girl, with whom he shared a previous dedication for sowing wild oats.

In all his pre-marital affairs Andrew's elder brother, Charles, had demonstrated as much energy, and far more discretion. When he went up to Trinity College, Cambridge, from Gordonstoun one girl described Charles as 'a sweet young virgin'. According to a widely held story, he surrendered this commodity to Lucia Santa Cruz, the Chilean Ambassador's daughter. She was an intelligent, sophisticated, and vivacious woman, three years his senior. She was a graduate student in history and Lord Butler, the Master of Trinity College, employed her as a research assistant to help him write his memoirs, *The Art of the Possible*. Since Lord Butler was opposed to Trinity College's policy of having a curfew on the undergraduates' rooms he may have lent her the key to the Master's Lodge.[7]

Cambridge legend also has it that the young prince climbed the walls of Newnham College so as to be with Sybilla Dorman, a fellow history undergraduate, and the daughter of the Governor General of Malta. But Charles squired Audrey Buxton, the daughter of one of his father's naturalist friends to the Trinity May Ball.

The list of the prince's girl friends during the decade between university and marriage reads as if he selected them from *Burke's Peerage*. They included: Leonora, the Duke of Westminster's daughter, and her sister, Jane, now the Duchess of Roxburghe; Lady Victoria Percy and her sister Lady Caroline, the Duke of Northumberland's two girls; Lady Cecil Kerr, daughter of the Marquess of Lothian; Lady Henrietta Fitzroy, daughter of the Duke of Grafton; Lady Charlotte Manner, the Duke of Rutland's daughter, and her cousin, Elizabeth; Angela, daughter of Lord Rupert Nevill; Lady Camilla Fane, the Earl of Westmorland's daughter; Lord Astor's daughter, Louise; Georgiana, Sir John Russell's child; and – above all – Lady Jane Wellesley, daughter of the eighth Duke of Wellington.

Charles and Jane had known each other since childhood. Born of the bluest of blue bloods, and thus accustomed to court life, she was attractive and self-possessed. She and the prince often visited her father's huge estate in Spain – which the Spanish government had given the first Duke to thank him for his part in the Napoleonic Wars. Press interest in Jane became so intense that she could not move without being followed by a posse of reporters. When she attended Morning Service at Sandringham village church as the Queen's weekend guest 10,000 people turned up to gawk. In fact everything was in favour of Lady Jane becoming a future queen except in two respects: Charles felt he was too young to settle down, and Lady Jane was not prepared to surrender her individuality and freedom.

Charles's next love, Davina Sheffield, a blond débutante, found the pressures of his courtship so intense that she ran off to work with orphans in Vietnam. When the Vietcong (who turned out to be even more of a threat than Fleet Street) forced her back home to England, the relationship with the prince was rekindled. After burglars brutally murdered her mother in the family's Oxfordshire home she became emotionally dependent on him. 'They were a couple obviously in love', remembered the prince's valet, 'I think that he would have married her but her past was suddenly revealed.'[8] An ex-lover, James Beard, an old-Harrovian boat designer, sold the story to the newspapers of how he had once lived with Davina. He provided details so intimate that no one could doubt his veracity – no matter how stringently they condemned his behaviour.

Of course, some girls did not mind the publicity engendered by the prince's attentions. If they had a past it did not matter, for these young ladies had enough sense to realize they lacked a royal future. Whilst serving aboard HMS *Minerva* Charles met Laura Joe Watkins, an American Admiral's daughter, who later turned up at a polo match in Deauville. Charles stopped seeing Fiona Watson, Lord Manton's daughter, when a jealous swain let it be known that she had revealed all in eleven pages of full colour to readers of *Penthouse* magazine. Others got equally short shrift when they failed to show public deference, as well as private decorum. Following a blazing row at the ball held to celebrate the Queen Mother's eightieth birthday, the heir's eighteen-month friendship with Anna Wallace abruptly ended.

What was the exact nature of Charles's relationship with all these young ladies one cannot say – for few will tell. 'I have fallen in love with all sorts of girls and fully intend to go on doing so', remarked the prince whilst still a bachelor.[9] He conducted his affairs privately, kindly, and with good manners. Charles had sense enough to accept the advice of his great uncle, Lord Mountbatten, never to consort with other men's wives – and wit enough to take up Mountbatten's offer to spend weekends at his house, Broadlands, to do so with their daughters.

The girls the prince chose for his trysts, which he preferred to hold in his private apartments at the Palace (that were off limits without permission even to the queen), or at the country houses of trusted friends, knew that the punishment for breaking confidences was not just battalions of reporters camping day and night on their doorsteps, but social ostracism for themselves and their families. Since the upper-class girls the prince liked were prepared to abide by his rules, and were particularly vulnerable to his censures, he was able to conduct most of his affairs in secret.

Even after the affairs were over they remained undisclosed, largely because the prince managed to part with most of his women on cordial terms. Often he brought them a farewell keepsake, such as a brooch. After she married a Chilean lawyer, Lucia Santa Cruz asked Prince Charles to be her first child's godfather. Following his own wedding to Lady Diana Spencer, Charles remained friends with Jane Wellesley, while Janet Jenkins, a Welsh girl whom he had met during helicopter training in Canada, on her own initiative returned all his letters. In sum the prince was able to handle the affairs of his heart with the kindness and decency that Edward VII possessed and Edward VIII so fatally lacked.

While such bodes well for his future performance as king, Charles faces two problems which were not present during the reigns of either Edward.

First, during the last few years public opinion has become much less tolerant of adultery – as Senators Gary Hart and John Tower, Prime Minister Uno, and Cecil Parkinson have all discovered to their costs. Perhaps the double standard about adultery has fallen victim to the feminist movement: it is hard, for instance, to envisage even so unmilitant a woman as the present Princess of Wales tolerating her husband's infidelities with the equanimity displayed by Queen Alexandra.

Second, during the last decade or so there has been nothing about the royal family, no matter how damaging or private, which the popular press would not publish. During the summer of 1936 when Edward VIII and Mrs Simpson cavorted aboard the *Nahlin* every English newspaper (including the communist *Daily Worker*) kept silence. But had that cruise taken place today, then within five minutes every capitalist rag on Fleet Street would be bruiting all the sordid detail with banner headlines and lurid photographs, and without much concern for veracity or good taste. In other words now a royal cannot conduct an extra-marital liaison without provoking a fire-storm of publicity. And if that liaison were not a heterosexual one then it seems likely that public opinion would be even less forgiving.

As we have seen, over the centuries the rules governing the monarchy have changed, and yet the human beings who make up the royal family have, like all of us, remained much the same. Of course, tradition and training make it hard to envisage a British monarch being stupid enough to try to regain the political powers his or her ancestors once wielded. But it is possible to contemplate someone whose inability to control their libido would wound or even destroy the crown. Thus if monarchy ever ends in Britain, might it be not with a political bang, but in the publicity of a royal affair?

NOTES

Place of publication is London unless stated otherwise.

I 'Be civil, I am the Protestant whore'

1 Tony Palmer, *Charles II: Portrait of an Age* (1979), 252.
2 Michel Foucault, *The History of Sexuality* (New York, 1980).
3 Samuel Pepys, *Diary*, ed. R. C. Latham and W. Matthews (Berkeley, 1970–83), 15 August 1665.
4 Giraldus Cambrensis, *Works*, ed. J. S. Brewer (1846), IV, 368.

II 'Nothing is more vile than to love a wife like a mistress'

1 C. Given-Wilson and A. Curteis, *The Royal Bastards of Medieval England* (1984), 36.
2 Christine Fell, *Women in Anglo-Saxon England* (Bloomington, 1984), 65.
3 M. C. Ross, 'Concubinage in Anglo-Saxon England', *Past and Present*, 108 (August 1985), 3–34.
4 William of Jamièges, in David C. Douglas and George W. Greenway, eds, *English Historical Documents*, 1042–1189 (London, 1981), II, 307–11.
5 Given-Wilson and Curteis, op. cit., 9, 99.
6 J. T. Appleby, *John King of England* (1960), 40.
7 F. Barlow, *William Rufus* (1985) 32.
8 Quoted in H. Montgomery Hyde, *The Love that Dare not Speak its Name* (Boston, 1970), 33.
9 Chilton L. Powell, *English Domestic Relations* (New York, 1917), 2.
10 Caroline Bingham, *Life and Times of Edward II* (1973), 44.

11 Ibid., 51.
12 Ibid., 58.
13 Ibid., 157.
14 D. Mancini, *The Usurpation of Richard III* (1969), 67.
15 Thomas More, *History of Richard III* (New Haven, Conn., 1963), II, 64.
16 Given-Wilson and Curteis, op. cit., 3–4.
17 More, op. cit., 64.

III 'Nothing but the English king's appetite'

1 Neville Williams, *Henry VIII and his Court* (1971), 46.
2 H. Savage, *The Love Letters of Henry VIII* (Denver, Colorado, 1949), 14.
3 J. Gairdner and R. H. Brodie, eds, *Letters and Papers, Foreign and Domestic, of the Reign of Henry VIII* (1862–1910), XIII, ii, 318.
4 Ibid., II, 395.
5 F. A. Mumby, *The Youth of Henry VIII* (Boston, 1913), 127.
6 C. Erickson, *Great Harry* (New York, 1980), 38–40.
7 David Loades, *The Tudor Court* (Totowa, New Jersey, 1987), 98.
8 Williams, op. cit., 50.
9 G. Mattingly, *Catherine of Aragon* (Boston, 1941), 123.
10 Williams, op. cit., 66.
11 *Calendar of State Papers, Venetian*, III, 455.
12 C. Erickson, *Mistress Anne* (New York, 1984), 26–38.
13 E. W. Ives, *Anne Boleyn* (Oxford, 1986), 23, 26.
14 Erickson, *Mistress Anne*, 48.
15 Ibid., 54, believes that he had; Ives, op. cit., 86, does not.
16 Gairdner and Brodie, op. cit., III, 2555.
17 Mumby, op. cit., 61.
18 *Calendar of State Papers, Venetian, 1527–33*, 824.
19 Ives, op. cit., 238.
20 Savage, op. cit., 33–4.
21 Ibid., 37, 47.
22 Edward Hall, *Hall's Chronicle* (1809), 758.
23 Gairdner and Brodie, op. cit., IV, 6114.
24 Ibid., 5679.
25 Jasper Ridley, *Henry VIII* (New York, 1985), 203.

26 Antonia Fraser, *Mary Queen of Scots* (New York, 1971), 257.

27 Ibid., 304.

IV   'Neither God, nor angel, but a man like any other'

1 Sir Anthony Weldon, 'The Court and Character of King James', in Sir Walter Scott, ed., *The Secret History of the Court of King James I* (1811), 1–2.

2 T. B. Macaulay, *History of England from the Accession of James II* (1858), I, 76.

3 Ibid., I, 410–12.

4 *Acts* VI: 15.

5 6/23, James to Charles and Buckingham, G. P. V. Akrigg, ed., *The Letters of King James VI and I* (Berkeley, 1984), 415–16.

6 Quoted in R. Lockyer, *Buckingham* (1981), 233.

7 H. Montgomery Hyde, *The Love that Dare not Speak its Name* (Boston, 1970), xviii; D. J. West, *Homosexuality* (1974), 36–43.

8 In the late 1960s a CBS/TV poll showed two-thirds of Americans regarded homosexuals with 'disgust, discomfort and fear'. Hyde, op. cit., xx.

9 F. Osborne, 'Traditional Memoryes of the Raigne of King James the First,' in Scott, op. cit., I, 276.

10 Caroline Bingham, *The Making of a King: the early years of James VI and I* (1968), 26.

11 Caroline Bingham, *James VI of Scotland* (1979), 17.

12 James I, *Basilikon Doron* (1944), 109; Akrigg, op. cit., 314–15.

13 Bingham, *James VI*, 34.

14 Karen Horney, *The Neurotic Personality of Our Time* (New York, 1964), 119.

15 Akrigg, op. cit., 98.

16 Bingham, *James VI*, 51–67.

17 Antonia Fraser, *King James of Scotland and I of England* (1974), 38.

18 A. L. Rowse, *Homosexuals in History* (New York, 1977), 54.

19 Akrigg, op. cit., 6–7.

20 Quoted by Fraser, op. cit., 39.

21 M. Lee, *John Maitland of Thirlestene and the Foundation of Stewart Despotism in Scotland* (Princeton, 1959), 79.

22 E. Williams, *Anne of Denmark* (1970), 62–4.

23 Lucy Aiken, *Memoirs of the Court of King Charles the First* (1833), I, 20.
24 Bingham, *James VI*, 124.
25 Ibid., 125.
26 Hyde, op. cit., 43–4.
27 J. Harington, *Nugae Antiquae* (1804), I, 390–7.
28 Rowse, op. cit., 58.
29 J. O. Halliwell, *Letters of the Kings of England* (1848), II, 131.
30 Harington, op. cit., I, 348.
31 Osborne, op. cit., I, 276. J. Nichols, *The Progresses, Processions and Magnificent Festivities of King James the First* (1828), III, 80.
32 Quoted in R. Lockyer, *Buckingham* (1981), 22.
33 Arthur Wilson, *The History of Great Britain, being the Life and Reign of King James the First* (1653), 147.
34 J. Chamberlain, *Letters* (Philadelphia, 1939), II, 142, 571.
35 Akrigg, op. cit., 431.
36 British Museum, Harleian Mss., 6986, 196.
37 Charles Carlton, *Charles I: the Personal Monarch* (1983), 123.
38 British Library, Egerton Mss, 1788, 24, 35.
39 C. W. Firebrace, *Honest Harry, Being the Biography of Henry Firebrace* (1932), 333, 341–2.
40 Ibid., 347.

V 'Never lay hands upon his sceptre'

1 Antonia Fraser, *Royal Charles* (New York, 1979), 180.
2 John Evelyn, *Diary*, ed. E. S. De Beer (Oxford, 1955), III, 246.
3 Fraser, op. cit., 9.
4 Christopher Falkus, *The Life and Times of Charles II* (Garden City, NY, 1973), 19.
5 Ibid., 117.
6 Edward Hyde, Earl of Clarendon, *History of the Great Rebellion* (Oxford, 1876), IV, 22–3.
7 Falkus, op. cit., 31; Evelyn, *Diary*, II, 562.
8 *A Collection of the State Papers of John Thurloe*, ed. Thomas Birch (1742), V, 645.
9 Maurice Ashley, *Charles II: Man and Statesman* (1971), 150.
10 Allen Andrews, *The Royal Whore: Barbara Villiers, Countess of Castlemaine* (1970), 44.
11 Ibid., 84.

12 Samuel Pepys, *Diary*, ed. R. C. Latham and W. Matthews (Berkeley, 1970–83), 7 December 1661.

13 Falkus, op. cit., 51.

14 Gilbert Burnet, *Burnet's History of my Own Time*, ed. O. Airy (Oxford, 1897), I, 307.

15 Pepys, *Diary*, 31 May 1662.

16 Ibid., 21 May 1662.

17 Tony Palmer, *Charles II, Portrait of an Age* (1979), 70.

18 Andrews, op. cit., 64.

19 Ibid., 104.

20 Fraser, *Royal Charles*, 240–2.

21 Andrews, op. cit., 77.

22 Pepys, *Diary*, 14 January 1668.

23 Palmer, op. cit., 165.

24 Evelyn, *Diary*, ed. De Beer, IV, 74.

25 Palmer, op. cit., 166.

26 Falkus, op. cit., 134–6.

27 'A Satyr on Charles II', *The Complete Poems of John Wilmot, Earl of Rochester*, ed. D. M. Vieth (New Haven, 1968), 61.

28 Palmer, op. cit., 75.

29 Fraser, *Royal Charles*, 413.

30 Ashley, op. cit., 147.

31 Andrew Marvell, *Poems and Letters* ed. H. M. Margoliots (Oxford, 1952), II, 194.

32 Palmer, op. cit., 70.

33 Pepys, *Diary*, 15 August 1665.

34 C. H. Firth and R. H. Rait, *Acts and Ordinances of the Interregnum, 1642–1660* (1911), 387–9; Lawrence Stone, *The Family, Sex and Marriage in England, 1500–1800* (New York, 1979), 329.

35 Antonia Fraser, *The Weaker Vessel* (1985), 446.

36 Quoted in ibid., 446.

37 Fraser, *Royal Charles*, 456.

38 J. P. Kenyon, *The Stuarts* (1958), 148.

39 Falkus, op. cit., 80.

40 Pepys, *Diary*, 7 October 1660.

41 Ibid., 24 June 1662.

42 Count de Grammont, *Memoirs* (1864), 274–82.

43 Fraser, *Weaker Vessel*, 454–7.

44 Pepys, *Diary*, 31 October 1668.

45 P. Earle, *The Life and Times of James I* (1972), 125.

46 J. Haswell, *James II* (1973), 24; F. C. Turner, *James II* (1948), 234.

47 L. B. Smith, *This Realm of England* (Boston, 1966), 286.

VI 'The frogs in the fable'

1 William B. Willcox, *The Age of Aristocracy* (Boston, 1966), 30.
2 J. M. Beattie, *The English Court in the Reign of George I* (Cambridge, 1967), 248.
3 M. Ashley, *The Stuarts in Love* (1963), 201.
4 Ibid., 210.
5 S. Baxter, *William III* (1966), 350.
6 J. Miller, *Life and Times of William and Mary* (1975), 48–9.
7 Ibid., 82.
8 H. and B. van der Zee, *William and Mary* (1973), 200–5.
9 Ashley, op. cit., 219.
10 Gila Curtis, *The Life and Times of Queen Anne* (1972), 43.
11 Ibid., 47.
12 R. Scott Stevenson, *Famous Illnesses in History* (1962), 202.
13 Curtis, op. cit., 34.
14 E. Gregg, *Queen Anne* (1980), 275.
15 P. Morand, *The Captive Princess: Sophia Dorothea of Celle* (New York, 1968), 96–7, 129.
16 H. Walpole, *Reminiscences*, ed. E. P. Taylor (Oxford, 1924), 29–30.
17 Ragnhild Hatton, *George I: Elector and King* (Cambridge, 1978), 50–1.
18 J. Beattie, op. cit., 241.
19 Lord Hervey, *Some Materials Towards the History of the Reign of George II*, ed. R. Sedgwick (1931), I, 11.
20 Beattie, op. cit., 248.
21 Ibid., 242.
22 *Lord Hervey's Memoirs*, ed. Romney Sedgwick (New York, 1952), 1.
23 Hatton, op. cit., 285.
24 Hervey, op. cit., 147–9.
25 Ibid., 10.
26 Ibid., 10.
27 'On a certain lady at court', quoted by Peter Quennell in *Caroline of England* (1939), 130.

28 C. F. Trench, *George II* (1973), 171.

29 Hervey, op. cit., 10–11.

30 Quennell, op. cit., 56.

31 Trench, op. cit., 190–1.

32 J. H. Plumb, *The First Four Georges* (1969), 89.

33 Trench, op. cit., 175.

34 Hervey, op. cit., 141.

35 Ibid., 12.

36 Trench, op. cit., 119–20.

37 Stanley Ayling, *George the Third* (New York, 1972), 16.

38 Hervey, op. cit., 145.

39 Anne Somerset, *Ladies in Waiting: From the Tudors to the Present Day* (New York, 1984), 223.

VII 'The damnedest millstones'

1 Roy Porter, 'Mixed Feelings: the Enlightenment and Sexuality', in Paul-Gabriel Bouce, *Sexuality in Eighteenth Century Britain* (Manchester, 1982), 10.

2 Roy Porter, *English Society in the Eighteenth Century* (Harmondsworth, 1982), 43.

3 J. H. Plumb, *The First Four Georges* (1969), 148.

4 Linda Colley, 'The Apotheosis of George III, Loyalty, Royalty, and the British Nation, 1760–1820', *Past and Present* (February, 1984), 120.

5 John Brooke, *King George III* (New York, 1972), 387.

6 Ibid., 420.

7 Ibid., 431.

8 Ibid., 40.

9 Ibid., 438.

10 C. Hibbert, *George IV; Regent and King: 1811–1830* (1975), 23.

11 Alan Palmer, *Life and Times of George IV* (1972), 20.

12 C. Hibbert, *George IV: Prince of Wales 1762–1811* (1972), 14.

13 Palmer, op. cit., 23.

14 Hibbert, *George IV: Prince*, 134–44.

15 Palmer, op. cit., 26.

16 Brooke, op. cit., 394–5.

17 Palmer, op. cit., 48.

18 Brooke, op. cit., 504.

19 Hibbert, *George IV; Prince*, 130–1.

20 Ibid., 134–44.
21 Carolly Erickson, *Our Tempestuous Day: a History of Regency England* (New York, 1986), 40.
22 Hibbert, *George IV; Regent and King*, 5.
23 Roger Fulford, *George the Fourth* (New York, 1963), 171–3.
24 Ibid., 132.
25 Palmer, op. cit., 181.
26 Philip Ziegler, *King William IV* (1972), 33.
27 Ibid., 51.
28 Ibid., 67.
29 Anne Somerset, *The Life and Times of William IV* (1980), 60–1.
30 Ibid., 69. .
31 Ziegler, op. cit., 106.
32 Somerset, op. cit., 81.
33 Elizabeth Longford, *Wellington: the Years of the Sword* (1969), 170.
34 Mollie Gillen, *Royal Duke: Augustus Frederick, Duke of Sussex* (1976), 202.
35 R. Fulford, *The Wicked Uncles: the Father of Queen Victoria and his Brothers* (New York, 1933), 226.
36 M. H. Abrams *et al.*, *The Norton Anthology of English Literature* (New York, 1974), II, 538.

VIII 'The king's loose box'

1 Anita Leslie, *Edwardians in Love* (1972), 220.
2 Philip Magnus, *King Edward VII* (1979), 370.
3 Ibid., 39.
4 James Brough, *The Prince and the Lily* (New York, 1976), 125.
5 Magnus, op. cit., 44.
6 Giles St Aubyn, *Edward VII: Prince and King* (New York, 1979), 50–3.
7 Magnus, op. cit., 69–75.
8 Ibid., 93.
9 Allen Andrews, *The Follies of King Edward VII* (1975), 108.
10 St Aubyn, op. cit., 153–6.
11 Andrews, op. cit., 108.
12 Virginia Cowles, *Gay Monarch, the Life and Pleasures of Edward VII* (New York, 1965), 55–6.

13 Keith Middlemas, *The Life and Times of Edward VII* (New York, 1972), 47.
14 Brough, op. cit., 44–6.
15 Ibid., 144.
16 Ibid., 146.
17 Cowles, op. cit., 116.
18 Andrews, op. cit., 144.
19 Brough, op. cit., 220.
20 Ibid., 332.
21 Christopher Hibbert, *The Royal Victorians* (Philadelphia, 1976), 165.
22 Magnus, op. cit., 285–6.
23 St Aubyn, op. cit., 379.
24 Leslie, op. cit., 229–30.
25 Ibid., 229–30.
26 Ibid., 101.
27 St Aubyn, op. cit., 384.
28 Cowles, op. cit., 124.
29 Middlemas, op. cit., 89.
30 Cowles, op. cit., 55–6.
31 St Aubyn, op. cit., 127.
32 Brough, op. cit., 192.
33 Ibid., 156, 168.

IX 'Things were done better in *my* day'

1 J. Bryan and Charles Murphy, *The Windsor Story* (New York, 1979), 306.
2 Frances Donaldson, *Edward VIII* (New York, 1978), 295.
3 Ibid., 64.
4 Ibid., 71.
5 Ibid., 75.
6 Ibid., 58–9.
7 Gloria Vanderbilt and Thelma Lady Furness, *Double Exposure: a Twin Autobiography* (New York, 1958), 278–9.
8 Bryan and Murphy, op. cit., 76.
9 Vanderbilt and Furness, op. cit., 282.
10 Bryan and Murphy, op. cit., 9.
11 The Duke of Windsor, *A King's Story* (New York, 1951), 257.

12 *Wallis and Edward: Letters, 1931–37*, ed. Michael Bloch (1986), 24.
13 Ibid., 72.
14 Vanderbilt and Furness, op. cit., 306.
15 The Duchess of Windsor, *The Heart has its Reasons* (New York, 1956), 187.
16 Bloch, op. cit., 98.
17 Ibid., 145, 156.
18 Donaldson, op. cit., 183.
19 Duke of Windsor, op. cit., 328.
20 Bloch, op. cit., 210–12.
21 Duke of Windsor, op. cit., 59.
22 Bryan and Murphy, op. cit., 58.
23 Duke of Windsor, op. cit., 81–3; Stephen Birmingham, *Duchess. The Story of Wallis Warfield Windsor* (Boston, 1981), 73.
24 Donaldson, op. cit., 47.
25 Duke of Windsor, op. cit., 110–12.
26 Bryan and Murphy, op. cit., 69.
27 Donaldson, op. cit., 172.
28 Christopher Hibbert, *Edward: the Uncrowned King* (New York, 1972), 80.
29 Bryan and Murphy, op. cit., 541; Alistair Cooke, *Six Men* (New York, 1978), 92.
30 Hibbert, op. cit., 6.
31 Donaldson, op. cit., 9.
32 George VI's cancer prompted a fatal heart attack during his sleep.
33 Duke of Windsor, op. cit., 24.
34 Ibid., 28.
35 The Duke of Windsor, *A Family Album* (1973), 101.
36 Brian Inglis, *Abdication* (New York, 1966), 25.
37 Donaldson, op. cit., 201, 311; Bryan and Murphy, op. cit., 392.
38 Ibid., 66, 69. My thanks to Mr Bryan and Mr Murphy for confirming this point about Mrs Dudley Ward's recollections in personal correspondence.
39 Ibid., 511.
40 Cooke, op. cit., 81.
41 Ibid., 583.

X 'Curtsy first, and then leap into bed'

1 J. Bryan and Charles Murphy, *The Windsor Story* (New York, 1979), 307.
2 Christopher Hibbert, *Edward, the Uncrowned King* (New York, 1972), 24.
3 Robert Lacey, *Majesty: Elizabeth II and the House of Windsor* (New York, 1977), 220.
4 Christopher Hibbert, *The Court of King James: the Monarch at work from Victoria to Elizabeth II* (New York, 1977), 220.
5 John Pearson, *The Ultimate Family: The Making of the Royal House of Windsor* (1986), 358–60.
6 Graham and Heather Fisher, *Strange and Fascinating Facts about the Royal Family* (New York, 1985), 246.
7 Anthony Holden, *Prince Charles* (New York, 1979), 229–37.
8 Stephen P. Barry, *Royal Service: my twelve years as valet to Prince Charles* (New York, 1983), 173.
9 Ibid., 166.

INDEX